Studying History

A practical guide to successful essay-writing, seminars, assignments and exams

Studymates

25 Key Topics in Business Studies
25 Key Topics in Human Resources
25 Key Topics in Marketing
Accident & Emergency Nursing
Business Organisation
Cultural Studies
English Legal System
European Reformation
GCSE Chemistry
GCSE English
GCSE History: Schools History Project
GCSE Sciences
Genetics
Hitler & Nazi Germany
Land Law
Memory
Organic Chemistry
Practical Drama & Theatre Arts
Social Anthropology
Social Statistics
Speaking Better French
Speaking English
Studying Chaucer
Studying History
Studying Literature
Studying Poetry
Understanding Maths
Using Information Technology

Many other titles in preparation

Studying History

A practical guide to successful essay-writing, seminars, assignments and exams

Robert Johnson
BA(Hons) PhD

www.**studymates**.co.uk

By the same author in this series
Hitler & Nazi Germany

First published in 2002 by Studymates, PO Box 2, Taunton, Somerset TA3 3YE

Telephone:	(01823) 432002
Fax:	(01823) 430097
Website:	http:www.studymates.co.uk

Note: The contents of this book are offered for the purposes of general guidance only and no liability can be accepted for any loss or expense incurred as a result of relying in particular circumstances on statements made in this book. Readers are advised to check the current position with the appropriate authorities before entering into personal arrangements.

Typeset by PDQ Typesetting, Newcastle-under-Lyme, Staffordshire.
Printed and bound by The Baskerville Press Ltd, Salisbury, Wiltshire.

Contents

Preface

In recent years, historians have been challenged by other academic disciplines to re-define their subject. This has not been a comfortable experience for those who have worked in history for many years, but the challenge should not have been unexpected. History has been developing as a discipline and profession for hundreds of years. Each succeeding generation has brought a fresh perspective to the process of historical research. New ideas have tested the existing approach to history, and in each case our subject has benefited from the experience. Historians have become more exacting, more rigorous than ever before. Nevertheless, the central essence of history is unchanging. It is a fascinating, often poignant and inspirational subject. In the wrong hands, history is a dangerous and bloody weapon. In the hands of a craftsman, it is a vehicle for enlightenment.

This guide will enable undergraduates and A-level students to understand the complex material, and vast historiography, of the study of history. Historical debate on the best method of study has reached critical mass and students need a quick reference guide to understand the strange web of methods, the bewildering array of new approaches and the difficult concepts. Increasingly, a clear understanding of these elements of history is demanded by examiners.

This guide will also enable the student to progress on a journey into the meaning of history, and, in easy stages, allow the student to gain a full understanding of how and why History is studied the way it is. Special features of this guide include:

1. previous and contemporary views of historians laid out clearly

2. an easy to follow 'how to' guide explained in short sections

3. a questioning approach to develop analytical techniques

4. advice on handling documents and archive work not included in other guides

The key to success in history is an analytical approach and the ability to conceptualise. Although this guide is aimed at undergraduates and A-level students, it will also be useful to third year university students and postgraduates who need a brief, and easy to follow, starting point for further study.

Acknowledgements

The inspiration and production of this book is thanks to several people. The first is Fred Reid, lecturer at Warwick University, who introduced the concept of historiography as a philosophy of history (rather than just what people had written about any historical topic) to many undergraduates in their final year. Colin Jones, now also at Warwick, made several MA students at Exeter rethink their comfortable assumptions about the way history was written, too. Another inspiration is Professor Richard Evans for his book *In Defence of History* (1998) which laid out the most sensible defence of the profession against the crisis-mongers for years. Students, especially those taking S-level (whom it has been my great pleasure to teach at Richard Huish College, Taunton), have proved the greatest challenge and the staunchest supporters for such a book as this. It is usually they who have given this book its form, did they but know it. My thanks are also due to Graham Lawlor for his confidence in me. This book is for all those who love history too, especially Dr Jackie Bennett, whom I am proud to call my colleague and my friend.

Robert Johnson

robertjohnson@studymates.co.uk

1

Themes and Problems in the Study of History

One-minute summary – Since history is a 'rational study of the past', it would seem a straightforward exercise to apply logic to the story of people, places and events that appeared in the past. However, attempts to define history have presented some problems. In a practical sense, arguments have developed over the generations about the best way to study the past. It is generally agreed that there is not one version of the past that is right, but that there are many different interpretations, just as there have been different responses to historical events from different eyewitnesses. To introduce you to this problem, and to present some ideas and solutions, this chapter begins by considering some ideas about history, before assessing the professions that appear to share the same skills that are required of a historian. Then, there is a discussion on the importance of debate and the exchange of ideas, and the importance of accuracy which distinguishes history from folklore and myth. Finally, there is a summary of historical skills. In this chapter you will learn about:

▶ the problems of defining history
▶ the skills required of a historian: the role of ideas and debate
▶ the problems of selecting and using evidence
▶ a summary of historians' skills

The problems of defining history

When asked 'What is history?' and 'Why is it important?' some students responded with the following comments:

'It is important for people to learn about their backgrounds and culture. If people are able to learn what has happened in the past,

9

they could learn from their ancestors' mistakes. By learning the skills of a historian, you are able to learn how to make a balanced view as you have to look at many sources to find the truth.'

'We can learn from the past how todays society, politics and economics developed'.

'The past teaches us what sort of governments systems work and why'.

'We study history to try to see things as other people saw them and interpret things in our own way'

'The study of history is an attempt to find patterns of meaning that help explain enduring human questions. Of all the fields of study, history can involve the most complex methods of research and analysis. History is an endeavour to understand humanity, first through the collection and discovery of facts, then through the critical interpretation of them.'

Each of these comments has something to offer. Although experienced historians might take exception to some of these remarks, it is encouraging to hear history regarded so highly. There are many important questions here. For example, there was mention of the search for truth, the desire to avoid the repetition of mistakes, the need to acknowledge that people in the past had different views from those our own time, and the need for certain skills of analysis which may be acquired, we can assume, through some form of 'learning' or training.

There is a sense of optimism about these definitions. Perhaps, it is surprising to learn then, that the very foundations of history have been challenged in the last decade. Nevertheless, historians have been fighting back to defend their subject, and as a result greater clarity has been achieved about how to study this fascinating area of human activity. This guide will take you through both the skills and the debates of history in order to show you how to apply them in a real and practical way.

The skills required of a historian

The similarities of journalism and history
Newspaper articles are interesting for more than just their content.

Often what is fascinating is not so much what they say, but how they say it. Look at their construction. In the first sentence or two, they have to say what has happened, to whom, when, and where. Newspaper articles have clear headings, or headlines, and the first sentences have to relate to the headline, or most dramatic statement. Then, the information, or story, is filtered into sections onto the page. It does not appear in a chronological order. The most attention-grabbing point, or the outcome, comes first. The less interesting information is given later.

Eyewitnesses also feature in newspaper articles. They lend a story authenticity. If there are no eyewitnesses, there are the comments of local officials, or sometimes even a neighbour or passer-by. Anonymity can be achieved without the loss of authority by expressions such as: 'highly placed sources say...'

Stories have to attract the interest of readers. Comments by the journalists or editors have to 'strike a chord'. Failure to do this means that the paper will not sell. In many ways, newspapers have to stir an emotion within us: shock, anger, dismay, pity or agreement. There is no doubt that journalists and editors are skilled craftsmen and women.

The historian as reporter

The historian works in a slightly different environment to the journalist, but there are similarities. Historians clearly write about events which occurred some time ago. In many cases, passions have cooled, and the historian is able to take the long view. The structure of what they say is also different. Where journalists have to put the key points in the first few lines, historians can distribute their ideas, dwell on issues with discussion, even lead their readers along a journey of exploration. Historians are not constrained by the need to report on just what has happened, but can reflect on the causes and consequences of events, and on the ideas of groups and individuals through time in far more depth.

Yet both the historian and the journalist make use of evidence from eyewitnesses and other, perhaps written, sources. Both have to use evidence to give their account authenticity; to make them believable.

The similarities of lawyer and historian

When a prosecuting lawyer stands up to address a court, he or she is expected to present a convincing case. There will already have been hours of painstaking work before the case has reached the court. A great volume of material will have been sifted, catalogued and cross-checked. The lawyer will use evidence, legal argument (the rules of law set down by previous cases) and produce a hypothesis of what happened, or of the accused's motives. It is a one-sided account. Where other views are acknowledged, they are always discredited. The aim is to win the case. The arguments will be conclusive, even if they are not strictly 'true'.

The historian as lawyer
The historian seems similar to the lawyer. Evidence is used to present a convincing case. Arguments, based on previous debates and scholarship, are evaluated and used. Hypotheses may be put forward. However, the arguments are less conclusive, and an argument that is too one-sided is less convincing than an even-handed approach. The evidence that a historian uses must be evaluated to see which ways it could be interpreted. It will not necessarily fit one interpretation. It may suggest many outcomes. The historian should be guided by this, and not be conclusive or dismissive of the different views and interpretations of others.

The detective
Journalists and lawyers use methods not dissimilar from historians, and they have much to teach us. However, there is another profession which holds a clue to the best method of a historian: the detective. Detectives have to process a wealth of evidence and decide what is relevant to the case and what is not. They have to compile a list of places, personalities and timings. They have to piece together the clues, and link several pieces of evidence with a hypothesis.

The hypothesis needs to be tested against each appropriate piece of evidence. Evidence which refutes the hypothesis means that the original theory has to be adjusted. As the clues are assembled, and linked, they seem to form 'leads'. Testing and delving deeper into the leads often produces more evidence which fits the hypothesis. More often than not, the leads turn out to be dead ends. The evidence dries up and appears to be irrelevant. Totally misleading clues, 'red herrings', are frustrating. Eventually, the detective will have to present his or her suggested answer, and all the evidence, to solve a crime. The ideas, and the evidence they have selected, will be rigorously tested in court.

The similarity of the detective and historian

The journalist and the lawyer are like historians in their presentation, but it is the detective who most resembles the scholar of the past. Much of the historian's labour is unseen. The search for clues, the cross-checking of information, the evaluation of interpretations and hypotheses are all done behind the scenes. It is sometimes hard work and time consuming. However, every historian has experienced the heady excitement of making a discovery; the connection between clues, or the revelation of one document among many that answers an apparently insoluble conundrum. A genealogist described the process of research as a 'bug' she had caught. Once you have been exposed to the idea, it is 'infectious'.

Why debate and discussion is valuable

If historians worked in isolation they would present narrow viewpoints, make many mistakes and repeat the same ideas. Historians engage in a dialogue with others. Interpretations are tested against the research and findings of fellow historians. Ideas are exchanged. Discussion with others helps to shape thoughts of our own. Explanation helps us to clarify what we really mean. We prioritise, and confirm our own understanding. Wider meanings are revealed through discussion, too.

Debates help us to realise that no one explanation is supreme. Other interpretations have some validity too. That is not to say that inaccurate or weak ideas areas are legitimate. These are soon weeded out by the rigour of debate. The consequences of having no dialogue at all can be serious. The following is a salutary example.

Example 1: the Fritz Fischer controversy

In 1919, after the First World War (1914-18), Germany was blamed for causing the conflict under the war guilt clause of the Treaty of Versailles. Many Germans felt that this was unfair. Throughout the inter-war years (1919-39), academics argued that all the European powers had shared a collective responsibility for the outbreak of the war.

After the Second World War (1939-45), German historians were even more determined to show that Hitler was an exceptional character in German history since he had aimed to start a war in 1939. There was, they argued, no continuity between the old German empire and the Nazis in Germany's foreign policy. This reinforced the impression that Nazism was an exceptional movement which had diverted Germany's otherwise peaceful approach to international relations. Proof of this was offered in the shape of Bethmann Hollweg, the German Chancellor before the First World War. It was alleged that Bethmann Hollweg was a civilian politician struggling to moderate the aggressiveness of an overbearing German military.

Fischer put forward a new thesis
It was Fritz Fischer who destroyed this idea in 1961. In that year he published *Griff nach der Weltmacht* (*The Bid for World Power*). Fischer argued that Bethmann Hollweg, far from being innocent in the drama of 1914, harboured his own aggressive designs. Not only had he wholeheartedly supported the Kaiser's war-mongering actions before 1914, but he had also drawn up the so-called September Programme. This plan, written in just one month after the outbreak of war in 1914, specified how Germany was aiming to dominate Europe by conquest. France was to be reduced to vassal status, Russia's borders were to redrawn far to the east. Belgium would become little more than a colony of Germany.

Fischer's ideas caused a storm of controversy in German academic circles. His thesis, it was argued, seemed to condemn Germans as responsible for all the aggression of the twentieth century. It made them appear to be either Nazi, or proto-Nazi (a version of Nazism before the invention of that ideology). As historian Michael Freund wrote in 1964: 'If it turned out to be the case that in 1914 the same thing happened as in 1939 [that the war was planned] then we could finally shut the book on German history; then Hitler would always have ruled over us and would go on ruling over us.'

The angry reaction to Fischer's ideas
Fischer was subjected to some harsh treatment from many of his German colleagues. He was accused of being a traitor. There were attempts to exclude him from archives and lectures. He was boycotted. But attempts to defeat his arguments failed because Fischer had provided documentary evidence for his ideas. Historians in Europe and America scrutinised these documents for themselves and sympathised with Fischer's view. Critics, however, focussed on the fact that Bethmann Hollweg was probably only expressing the ideas of the Royal court and not his own perspective when he drew up the September Programme. In addition, they argued that, under the rare-

fied conditions of war, with Germany fighting for its life, it was not surprising that some vision of Europe after Germany's victory would be expressed in an extreme form.

The weaknesses of the critics
However, the critics were determined to ignore the evidence. The September Programme was found to have been drafted by Bethmann Hollweg's assistant, Kurt Riezler, as early as August 1914 – just two weeks after the outbreak of war. Germany was fighting Russia and France at the same time because of their aggressive war plan, the so-called Schlieffen Plan, which had specified the automatic invasion of neutral countries like Belgium, and an unprovoked attack on France, at the moment that Russia and Germany went to war. Fischer responded to his critics by carrying out research on the period between 1911 and August 1914. His second book, *War of Illusions* (1969), demonstrated that there was complete continuity in Germany's aims throughout this period. However, the controversy did not end there.

Problems with the evidence remain unresolved
Although some archives from the period 1911 to 1914 were destroyed in the Second World War, Professor John Rohl is dismayed that some evidence has been falsified or withheld from academic scrutiny. He cites, for example, Admiral Müller's comment in 1914 that 'the government has succeeded very well in making us appear as the attacked', but in 1965, the published version read 'the completely justified claim is made that we are the attacked'.

Another example concerns the Riezler diaries. When Bethmann Hollweg's assistant, Kurt Riezler, died in 1955, his brother became the keeper of the diaries. During the Fischer controversy, it was claimed by those who had seen or heard parts of the original diaries, that Riezler described Bethmann Hollweg as someone who desired war with Russia. He was, as the Germans would say, kriegslustig. When the diaries were published in 1972, it gradually became apparent that these descriptions were simply not there. Bethmann Hollweg, far from wanting war, seemed to be fatalistic and philosophical. Bernd Sosemann, a young academic, tried to gain access to the original diaries for 8 years, and when he did he was critical of the transcriptions. In addition, it was discovered that only the diaries from 1914 were there, even though Riezler kept a diary from 1907. At the time of writing, this mystery has not been solved.

The final piece of the jigsaw?
Nevertheless, the final piece of evidence has been the discovery of the
December 1912 War Council document. It appears that the Kaiser was
eager for a war in 1912, but was persuaded to postpone the 'great fight'
for 'one and half years' so that the German navy could increase its
strength. This time period brings the planned outbreak of war to the
summer of 1914, precisely when the crisis began. As more documents
appear, they seem to reinforce the Fischer thesis that war was
planned. John Rohl believes that there can now be little doubt about
the aggressive intentions of the ruling elites between 1912 and 1914.
This is confirmed by the record of Rudolf von Valentini, head of the
imperial civil cabinet, who wrote in his diary how, at a dinner attended
by the Kaiser and the imperial princes, all of them were 'full of
Kriegslust'.

Conclusions about the Fischer controversy
Fischer had challenged an assumption about the causes of the First
World War, but in doing so, he had also destroyed the idea that
Germany had pursued an essentially peaceful foreign policy until the
1930s. The reaction to Fischer was extraordinary. However, through
continued debate and discussion, through the scrutiny of other
sources, and through the corroboration of different accounts, a more
accurate picture of Germany's role in the outbreak of the First World
War has emerged.

This does not mean that the subject has been closed. The debates
will continue. Ideas will be exchanged. New evidence will come to
light and new interpretations of existing material will be offered.
This makes history an exciting and dynamic subject.

Example 2: the Gentry Debate

A more heartening example of how dialogue can help is the so-called
Gentry Debate. This concerns the origins of the English civil war
(1642-45). Historians who argued that the momentous events of the
civil war must have had deep-seated causes, pointed to the rise of the
gentry as a key factor. This class, they argued, consisted of the 'new
rich'; men who had made money from commerce now wanted a share
of political power. Denied this power-sharing by the Stuart tyrant
Charles I, they rebelled in 1642. The whole basis of the argument
rested on the belief that the gentry were rich, or becoming richer,
and as a result, their aspirations to rule grew ever stronger.

The contribution of local history

However, within a few years, research by local historians in many small county archives throughout England and Wales revealed a more complex pattern. Some gentry, they agreed, were becoming richer in the 1630s. However, just as many were impoverished, or just stayed the same. This led to a new discussion on which members of the gentry had led the attack on the king, and, ultimately, to more questions about the causes of the civil war which were quite unconnected with the gentry. The debate had developed and provoked new thoughts on this important area of British history. The conclusion was that the 1630s were far more complex, and rich in controversy, than originally assumed.

The problems of selecting and using evidence

One of the greatest difficulties the historian will face is the question of evidence. Historians working in the field of ancient history quite often face the problem of fragmentary evidence. Sometimes very little evidence has survived to our own time. From a limited collection, the historian may have great difficulty in reconstructing the past. For historians of more modern periods, the opposite can be true. There can be so much material that selection becomes a real trial. Questions arise, such as:

1. 'On what basis should the evidence be selected?'
2. 'Will selection lead to distortion?'
3. 'Can every view be represented?'
4. 'How should atypical evidence be presented?'

However, there can be little doubt that the historians' use of evidence sets them apart from propaganda and folklore. Handling evidence requires skill, and a sense of professionalism, which seeks to avoid the pitfalls of partiality or 'bias', is also a hallmark of the historian.

The historian can dispel myths

Historians can be useful in exposing myths as fraudulent and misleading. Historians will also challenge those who try to create and exploit myths for their own ends.

The film 'Gallipoli'

The actor-director Mel Gibson has appeared in two films which created myths. In the film called *Gallipoli*, the film-makers attempted to portray the experiences of two young Australians in a military campaign of the First World War. The battle for the Gallipoli peninsula took place in 1915, and involved Turkish forces in defence, with British, Australian and New Zealand troops in the attack. The film shows the difficult conditions the soldiers faced; snipers, machine gun fire and artillery bombardments. In a battle scene, the Australian soldiers are shown to be brave, but needlessly sacrificed by a ruthless British commander. The British officer is shown ordering the Australians into the attack, even though Turkish resistance is murderously strong, in order to support a British attack further up the coast. However, a signaller reports that the British were not resisted and had sat down on the beach to drink tea. This comment is made between scenes of attacks by Australians who are mown down by Turkish machine guns. The film-makers make you feel that the Australians were killed without reason, and that the British sacrificed them. But this is a myth.

In reality the British contingent at Gallipoli was far greater in size than the Australian one. British troops had landed at Cape Helles and suffered heavy casualties as they came ashore. At Anzac Bay, fresh landings by Australians and New Zealanders failed to make much headway. New landings by the British at Suvla Bay met a similar fate. All the fighting at Gallipoli was at close quarters, and demanded immense courage. British casualties were higher than those of the Australians, but no country's army had a monopoly on bravery. Eyewitnesses recorded their respect for 'Johnny Turk' because Turkish soldiers were as determined and brave as the allies. This begs the questions:

1. What did the film-makers intend by their portrayal?

2. Why did they choose to give one interpretation which wasn't based on fact?

3. The description of British troops drinking tea in their landings at Suvla, whilst Australians were massacred, is a fabrication; why was this done?

The film of Wallace and 'Braveheart'
A second film may help us to answer these questions. In *Braveheart*, the Scottish warrior, William Wallace, is shown organising resistance to the English king Edward Longshanks. Wallace is portrayed as heroic, resourceful and clever. The English are shown to be tyrannical, ruthless and cruel. The Scottish nobles are presented as a divided, and often treacherous group who are also quite inept.

The film-makers altered the chronology of real events in order to create a 'message'. Wallace is trapped and captured. As he is tortured and dies, Edward apparently dies at the same moment, in the same agony. In fact, their deaths were separated by many years.

There are other changes. In the film, Wallace meets Edward's French Queen and they form a close relationship. In reality, they never met. Historian Dr Sandy Grant was unimpressed by the film-maker's version. He believed the real story was much more interesting than the 'Hollywood' approach. The question remains: what was the intention of those who wished to alter reality?

In one way, it may have been to create a dramatic effect. A sense of crisis makes the audience want the main character of the story to succeed. A villain of the story shows the main character in an even more heroic light. The film-makers are, after all, in the business of 'selling' stories. Yet the difficulty is the subject matter. The films cited here pretend to be reality. The characters and the places have real names, but the story is false. Audiences leave the cinema thinking they have seen a recreation of real history. That both films carry the same nationalistic themes, and are made by the same film-maker, leaves one deeply suspicious of their motives.

How history can be made to serve ideologies
When the Soviet Union – and Nazi Germany – examined history, they decided to rewrite those sections that did not fit their ideological agendas.

(a) In the Soviet Union, economic forces were used to explain all world history. Society was divided into categories: those who supported the people, and the counter-revolutionaries, who did not.

(b) The same simple, black-and-white division of society was used by the Nazis; but the criterion there was race. The Nazi history of

Germany, and the world, was, they argued, a story of a struggle between good Aryans and evil Jews, or, as the Nazis regarded them, half-breeds like the Slavs. The casualties these regimes inflicted on their own populations were horrific.

The misuse of history to reinforce an ideological agenda has dramatic but incredibly dangerous consequences. On the other hand, historians are powerful individuals who can challenge the myth-makers. Through writing, and speaking, historians are the champions of truth.

Historians throughout history

Historians of the past
History is a subject that has evolved. Until the eighteenth century, reality and myth tended to overlap:

1. Collectors of ancient artefacts, or antiquarians, were concerned only with their objects, and were less interested in their context.

2. The singer-historians of the Middle East, who passed epic tales from generation to generation, and embellished their songs with supernatural wonders.

3. The early narratives of history contained a mixture of myth and reality. In England, for example, stories of King Arthur were as real as the Norman Conquest.

Since the nineteenth century, history has become more 'scientific'. In other words, it has established methods. Often, those methods have been challenged and debated, until, in the last decade the motives of historians themselves have been under fire. Later on we will review these debates, and explain how they were resolved.

Historians today
History has taken on many techniques from other disciplines. Anthropology, sociology and political science, for example, have given us additional tools of analysis. This has enriched the study of history, and improved its presentation.

History is now a broad discipline. It embraces many forms. Cultural history, gender history, the history of medicine and environmental history are all recent arrivals. It is also a discerning subject, and historians have to measure up to a rigorous standard. To be a historian requires training, and historians need a certain quality of rugged endurance.

A checklist

So far we have established:

1. Evidence is essential to support or authenticate ideas.

2. Hypotheses can be formed to link evidence and ideas, but should be tested by all the evidence that is available.

3. Historians are not solely concerned with events, or people, but they are expected to make comment on the past, and to evaluate it. However, they have to avoid one-sidedness by acknowledging other interpretations.

4. Historians engage in debate to broaden and test their ideas, and to extend their knowledge of a period of the past.

5. Historians must have a command of good presentation techniques in order to communicate their ideas efficiently.

6. The ability to write to a high standard is a valuable asset.

7. Reading is essential and historians are expected to have an awareness of subjects beyond their own immediate field of interest. A knowledge of the existing scholarship and new discussions is often acquired through journals and monographs.

Tutorial: helping you learn

Progress questions

1. Give your own short definition of history and explain why it is important to study it. One paragraph will be enough. Use no more than 100 words. This will help to clarify your impressions of this first chapter.

2. What did the Fritz Fischer debate do for the study of the causes of the First World War?

3. What are the problems of selecting and using evidence?

Discussion points

1. Why do historians concentrate on more than just 'facts' when considering what happened in the past?

2. If interpretation helps a historian, how do we know which interpretation is right? Does it actually matter?

Practical assignment

From the history that you have studied to date, can you identify the motor causes of up to six key events? You could choose, for example, the First World War, or why women have had a 'subordinate' role for so long in western society.

Study and revision tips

1. Make a list of the skills identified as those required by a historian in this chapter.

2. Note that ideas and arguments have been just as important to historians as 'facts'.

3. Look out for myths and propaganda. Try to identify the reasons for these phenomena.

4. Refer back to the checklist at the end of the chapter. Use a highlighter pen to pick out the most important points. Tick those that you think you will need to work on.

The Ideas of Ancient and Classical Historians

One-minute summary – It is important to know how history has been studied. You can then apply the findings of other historians to your own studies. Be aware of what past historians were trying to achieve, and the pitfalls they identified. Don't judge the historians of the past solely by the standards of historical methods today: try to appreciate the purpose of historical writing in each period. This chapter begins by explaining how classical historians of the ancient period struggled with causation in history, and how they tried to use history to teach contemporary lessons. In the 'Dark Ages', clerical historians set out to reinforce the Christian message. In the medieval period there was an emphasis on the annals, or chronicles, which listed events but not always with accuracy. The Renaissance in the fifteenth century saw a return to classical models but adapted to new political situations. The troubled seventeenth century in Britain produced a determination to cite documentary evidence to justify historical accounts. We should also acknowledge traditions of historical writing outside Europe. In this chapter you will learn about:

▶ the Greeks and Romans – history in the service of politics
▶ classical rhetoric as a tool of persuasion
▶ Christian history as evidence of a divine plan
▶ the Renaissance revival of the classical model
▶ the impact of seventeenth century historical ideas
▶ the strong historical tradition outside Europe.

The Greeks and Romans: history in the service of politics

Herodotus (c.484 - c.430 BC) aimed to record 'achievements'

Herodotus wrote one of the earliest works of recorded history, *The Histories*. In modern parlance, he was a military and diplomatic historian. He aimed to record the 'astonishing achievements' of his people, the

Greeks, and to show how they managed to defeat those who had tried to conquer his homeland, namely the Persians.

The style of his text suggests that Herodotus meant the *Histories* to be read out loud, as a speech perhaps. This would have been in keeping with the traditions of his day. Across southern Europe and the Middle East, bards composed and recited the history of their land, their heroes and their people. Song, or poetry, was an aid to memory, and the practice had begun long before written records were made. Indeed, poems and songs may have been the earliest form of human history. They recorded all-important family lineage (to legitimatise a claim to land, for example), key events in the history of a community, or its achievements. In this sense, history had begun to both inform and entertain.

The content of Herodotus' work: the causes of war

Herodotus wrote about the rise of the Persian Empire under Cyrus (559-529 BC), the causes of the Persian wars (490-479 BC), and the defeat of Emperor Xerxes' attempts to conquer the Greeks (480-479 BC). He also observed how, once the Persian threat had passed, the Greeks fought amongst themselves. The city state of Athens was attacked by Sparta. During this conflict, the Athenians made an alliance with their old enemies the Persians. Nevertheless, Athens eventually lost the so-called Peloponnesian war (431-404 BC).

However, Herodotus gave us more information than just the narratives of these conflicts. He often sought to explain motives of the states and their leaders. For example he showed the importance of revenge, and of duty, in Greek culture. Myths, customs, beliefs systems and geographical details were also acknowledged as influential factors affecting key events. He also hinted at the central role played by the gods in the Greeks decision-making, even though he made no judgement on this as a factor in how history 'works'.

Causes in history

Herodotus used eyewitness statements to describe events, often citing his sources. However, he did not always accept a version of events without question:

1. He led his readers through a discussion of each point.
2. He presented contrary viewpoints, or supporting sources.
3. He offered an explanation for these similarities and differences.
4. He also tried to clarify the source of legends, or to explain them.

Detlev Fehling argued (*Herodotus and his Sources*, 1989) that Herodotus may have invented some 'eyewitnesses' or sources to make his arguments more plausible. The strangest tales may have been to entertain, or perhaps to make the central characters appear more heroic, in the same style as the epic poems *The Iliad* and *The Odyssey*. However, Herodotus seemed to share with many of his countrymen some scepticism about the influence of the gods in shaping events. He had shown the importance of oral history and tried to offer a balanced approach where conflicting accounts existed. His emphasis on enquiry, testing sources, and discussion, prompted Cicero – a Roman historian – to describe Herodotus as the 'father of history'.

Thucydides (c.460-400 BC) and the truth about the Peloponnesian war

Thucydides was an Athenian military officer who had served and fought in the Peloponnesian war. He wanted to establish the truth about the war – its causes, the decisions that leaders had taken, and what had been said. He claimed to write impartially, offering sources from both sides of the conflict. He tried to reproduce speeches made by the leaders involved, and offered an analysis of how military leaders react under the stress of war.

However, the explanation of human behaviour ends there. There were no references to the myths, or to the gods, as Herodotus had made. Thucydides admitted that the speeches that he reproduced were not necessarily accurate either. He wrote that in some cases it was:

> 'difficult to carry them word for word in one's memory, so my habit has been to make the speakers say what was in my opinion demanded of them by the various occasions, of course adhering as closely as possible to the general sense of what they really said'.

In today's terms we might call Thucydides' work a docu-drama rather than a history. However, Thucydides offered a version of history that offered a narrative of events, interspersed with eyewitness accounts, and unambiguous conclusions.

Polybius (c.200-118 BC) and the origins of political history

Polybius was one of the most famous writers of the Roman period, although born a Greek. His works, the *Histories*, were divided into 40 volumes written over his lifetime. As an exile in Italy, he wrote his books with both Greek and Roman readers in mind, but he was clearly impressed with Roman achievements. He got to know many of the Roman elites, and went with Roman troops to Carthage before travelling along the north African coast.

Polybius regarded history as a practical exercise. He meant to show, through a record of recent events, how the Roman political constitution had enabled the empire to grow and develop. This, and an understanding of causation in history, would give the reader a practical guide to good government. For the Greeks, eclipsed by the spread of the Roman empire, this was to be (thought Polybius) a useful set of instructions. He specified in book 12 that his *Histories* were for the benefit of 'ordinary people'. By this he meant people likely to be engaged in the practical business of politics, rather than the philosophers.

Polybius' methods emphasised political lessons
Polybius concentrated on military, political and diplomatic history, using his contacts amongst the civilian and military elites of Rome. Unlike Thucydides, he was at pains to elaborate on his own observations of geography and culture. He also laid down a guide to studying history. He believed that history consisted of:

1. the collection and examination of written sources

2. a survey of the relevant geography

3. an explanation of political structure and its workings through interviews of those with experience.

Polybius also offered long explanations of military campaigns, the leadership of certain officers and the uses of the various arms. The performance of men under battle conditions also fascinated him. As an ex-cavalry officer himself, this was perhaps not surprising.

Nevertheless, Polybius' first concern was to give a thorough explanation of political success. Unfortunately he tended to give undue emphasis to political structure, rather than to the influence of individuals – in stark contrast to his assessment of military success where he viewed leadership as important. However, he rather played down the role of the gods and fate, whilst acknowledging that these did play a useful role in ensuring the control of the people. Nevertheless, the role of individuals in shaping history – and the role of ideologies – have remained common themes for historians ever since.

Classical rhetoric as a tool of persuasion

How Cicero used rhetoric to judge the present and the past

The chief characteristic of Roman historians was their desire to pronounce on political behaviour. Their method was persuasion through rhetoric. On the face of it, they presented two opposing views, and weighed up the pros and cons of each; in reality they always had one view in mind. While appearing to be totally balanced and neutral, the Roman historian could cleverly convince his audience of his own preferred view. This technique had, of course, existed in Greece, but proved enormously influential in history when Roman works were reappraised and republished in the fourteenth and fifteenth centuries.

Cicero (106-43 BC) was a Roman politician who survived an assassination attempt. He was recalled from exile by popular demand, partly through his skill in rhetoric. Among his works was *On the Orator*, which described the importance of judgement and comment over and above the dry recording of events. Cicero was less concerned with what happened in the past, than with what might be learned about politics, and how this could be conveyed persuasively. Ironically, he lost the rhetorical game, since he was murdered for failing to commit himself to a political faction led by Mark Antony.

Livy used rhetoric

Livy (Titus Livius, c. 64 BC to 17 AD) also used the technique of rhetoric to teach political lessons, and to emphasise the importance of patriotism. His massive work, 142 volumes on *The History of Rome from its Foundation*, was supposed to cover 800 years of history, but sadly not all of the books have survived. Nevertheless, his version of events was to prove resilient, enjoying some popularity during the Italian Renaissance (c.1370-1520). Livy was not afraid to use legends, such as the myth that Rome was founded by Romulus and Remus, in order to reinforce a sense of pride. Various gods also play a part in Rome's fortunes. To Livy, style and language mattered more than a bland chronicle of events. For him, persuasion by a well-composed argument was essential.

The impact of Polybius, Livy and Cicero

The Roman historians shared the desire to instruct through history. Their key technique was rhetoric. If eyewitnesses were unavailable, then it was acceptable to give an approximation of what they might have said, especially if this served the idea of a greater truth. Polybius turned out to be more popular to later generations than Thucydides because of his emphasis on learning political lessons.

The practical challenge of managing states appealed to Renaissance scholars like Leonardo Bruni and Nicolo Machiavelli. Fate and the gods were acknowledged as tools in the service of the states, and in the construction of myths. These classical scholars were fascinated by the performance of the empire, and by the causation of the events they observed. They offered judgements and solutions. The emphasis of their work was always on 'persuasion'. Given the responses of students in chapter one, this appears to have had a lasting influence.

Christian history as evidence of a divine plan

New traditions emerged with the rise of Christianity

The collapse of the Roman empire spanned many decades. Indeed, it could argued, as did Edward Gibbon in *The Decline and Fall of the Roman Empire* (1776), that the Roman empire only finally collapsed with the fall of Constantinople to the Muslim Turks in 1453. In western Europe, Roman ideas and culture were overtaken by both indigenous peoples, and by new migrants from central and eastern regions.

The decades following the collapse of the Roman empire have been called the Dark Ages. This term has been somewhat discredited. It used to be assumed that it referred to a regression from Roman civilisation to the barbarian cultures of the eastern invaders. Now the term is used to mean the lack of clear evidence about what happened after the fall of the Roman empire in the west.

However, the period was not devoid of historical records or method:

1.   Eusebius, the bishop of Caesarea from 313 AD, wrote an account of how the Roman empire in the east and the theology of Christianity were inextricably linked. Whilst this worldly view was criticised by St Augustine in the 22 volumes of *City of God* (c.412-27, covering the creation to 417), he claimed that the empire had not collapsed because it had become Christian; in fact it had been an agency for good.

2.   In Britain, the earliest surviving manuscripts of the *Anglo-Saxon Chronicles* date from around 890 AD, with Nennius' *History of the Brit-*

ons estimated at c.830. Like many Christian histories, they began with the Creation in order to establish continuity. However, perhaps the most influential source of British history from this period was the Venerable Bede's *Ecclesiastical History of the English People*, written about 731.

The Christian tradition aimed to broadcast the Word of God

The Christians were successful in spreading their ideas across the European continent, often in the teeth of pagan violence or persecution. It was not surprising that Christian chroniclers recorded their histories in a positive light. Their aim was not simply to highlight their achievements. They wanted to persuade non-believers to adopt their faith, and to confirm the religion amongst existing Christians.

The key problem for Christian historians, though, was how to resolve man's actions and God's will. God's plan for the universe was, according to the Gospels, a divine mystery to be revealed to man only at the time of God's choosing. Yet Christian theology acknowledged the role of human agency in shaping an individual's destiny. According to these histories, those who conformed to God's will would benefit, but there were situations where men had chosen to follow their own paths. The Bible was seen as an instructive history, which heavily influenced these writers, and moral lessons were drawn from the events they described.

The Venerable Bede (c. 672-735), a respected and influential scholar

Bede was a monk and scholar of Northumbria, one of the seven Anglo-Saxon kingdoms in England. Through his monastery, he had close contacts with churches in Europe. He used these contacts to acquire sources and other scholars' works. Bede was industrious, producing numerous books, for example on the lives of saints. However, arguably his greatest legacy was to establish a chronology of world history with the birth of Christ as the start of the Christian calendar. The BC/AD nomenclature was adopted throughout Europe because of Bede. But Bede did more than just create a list of world events: he aimed to use history as a means of promoting his Northumbrian version of Christianity.

Throughout his work, Bede referred to his sources. He credited others who had carried out research before him, namely Abbot Albinus of Canterbury, a priest called Nothelm from Kent who had visited the archives in Rome, and Bishop Daniel of the West Saxons (Wessex). Bede also used countless eyewitness accounts, faithfully recording those who had testified to miraculous events.

The strengths and weaknesses of Bede's accounts
Bede tended to judge the fortunes of rulers, or their decisions, on the basis of their faith. Good rulers, in the eyes of God, tended to succeed. Bede thus tended to play down, or ignore, the successes of pagan kings. This has given us a misleading impression that the transition of England to a Christian country was a smooth process. Northumbria, and Bede's own kingdom of Bernicia, was the rival of Mercia, and there are references to the superiority of Northumbria throughout his *Ecclesiastical History*.

However, like the Classical scholars of Greece and Rome, Bede felt that he served a higher truth, one which required him to do more than simply list events. His purpose was to promote the Christian message. History was just one means to this end, and can be seen as part of an arsenal which also included the Anglo-Saxon translation of John's Gospel (surely a historical inspiration, with its opening line: 'In the beginning was the Word...'). This would account for his criticism of pagan monarchs, or of the Welsh Christians who had refused to accept the brand of Roman theology Bede himself favoured.

There were other problems with Bede's work, too. The dating of events between 449 and 538 were dependent on the *Anglo-Saxon Chronicles*, but these chronologies were often inaccurate having been recorded by word of mouth long before any written record was made.

Bede's influence is controversial
Bede's contribution to history may have been misunderstood by later generations, who focused on his literary worth. His main contribution was to make commentaries on the existing chronologies. However, his impact belonged to a particular period, the struggle for Christian supremacy in England. Due to the unreliability of his dating, scholars of early Saxon England have had to rely more on archaeology and the fragmentary remarks of indigenous Britons, such as Gildas (writings c.540). John Warren (*History and the Historians*, 1999) believes that English historians were more influenced by the traditions of the *Anglo-Saxon Chronicles* and the annals (lists used to calculate the date of Easter), than by Bede.

However, it would be fair to say that Bede's extraordinary industry, and his attempts to record a positive and instructional version of Anglo-Saxon England based on the Christian faith, was influential. It also established the legitimacy of Saxon monarchy into the early medieval period.

The Renaissance revival of the classical model

The medieval tradition superseded by the Renaissance
The first of the *Anglo-Saxon Chronicles* has been dated to the reign of King Alfred (871-899). They followed the pattern of the annals in recording events of local political significance, or environmental events. Although this approach lasted until the twelfth century in England, the method was limited to listing a chronology but was periodically embellished with explanations of how events reflected God's will. Much of this was because the chronicles were composed by the clergy.

However, by the 1200s, Britain saw the growth of towns and urban administration. The new chronicles were increasingly secular in character. This trend was also evident elsewhere in western Europe. By the late fourteenth century we can discern a new approach to the recording of events, which was particularly marked in Italy. Despite some disagreement among historians about the right description of the period, the term 'Renaissance' is the one most often used.

The Renaissance in Italy
Arnold Toynbee, author of *A Study of History* (1973), remarked that the Italian Renaissance was an incubus (a dead spirit) of the Roman period, which stifled the development of a truly fresh approach to the modern world. This judgement seems quite harsh.

Francesca Petrarca (1304-74), a poet and scholar in Florence, rediscovered classical works of history and literature with great enthusiasm. Petrarca had a passion for ancient Rome because the ruins he had observed indicated past glories. The city-state of Florence seemed to parallel the rise of the Roman republic, and Florentine scholars and artists joined in the chance to promote their own city's prestige. There was a passion for research into classical documents for religious reasons; some hoped to find out more about the true church of Christ which was contemporaneous with the Roman writers. The interest in the classical writers led to a rebirth of the Roman style of historical writing too, with the emphasis Polybius had placed on teaching moral lessons and good political style.

Leonardo Bruni (c. 1370-1444) revived the classical style
Bruni departed from the medieval chroniclers' annals in his *History of the Florentine People*. He examined sources and revealed that Florence had not been founded by Caesar, destroyed by the Goths, or refounded by Charlemagne. However, Bruni mistakenly believed that the famous Baptistry of Florence had been a temple of Mars, even though it had only been built in the twelfth century.

Bruni was vague on political conflicts in the past, but eager to show that republicanism was a superior form of government. He attributed the fall of the Roman empire to the rise of imperial rulers. In the same way, he explained the rise of the Italian city-states in his own period to the waning of imperial rule south of the Alps. Bruni's style was copied by Flavio Biondo in *Decades of History* (1439-50) which explained the fall of the Roman empire as a result of barbarian invasions. Like Bruni, Biondo identified a period called the 'Middle Age' between the classical period and the modern period; something which medieval chroniclers had found impossible to appreciate.

The lasting influence of the Renaissance

There can be little doubt that the revival of classical models of writing history helped to redevelop history as a craft. There were still problems, of course. The Renaissance historians had the problem of trying to adopt the classical writers' political message and pagan interpretation of events through the pantheon of gods, with the modern political situation in Italy, and with the monotheistic tradition of Christianity where God's direction was paramount.

The development of humanist philosophy in the Renaissance has been exaggerated thanks to the efforts of German nineteenth-century commentators. It is all too easy to assume that Renaissance thinkers turned their backs on Christianity. This is not the case; it artificially anticipates the Enlightenment of the eighteenth century. Instead, Renaissance scholars seem to have selected from the classical writers those aspects which suited their modern purpose. For example rhetoric could be used in modern Italian politics, and political lessons highlighted. References to the Roman period gave Renaissance authors an authority. After all, the Roman empire had been a long lasting, successful and politically powerful structure of which fifteenth-century Italians could be proud. Machiavelli's writings, such as *The Prince* (1516), confirm this approach.

The impact of seventeenth-century historical ideas

The seventeenth century historiography has been overlooked

It can be hard to find accounts of the late sixteenth and seventeenth centuries in any works on historiography. This is a pity. A student could be
forgiven for thinking that there was a direct link between the seculari-
sation of the Renaissance and the Enlightenment of the eighteenth
century.

However, the political struggles in Britain during the early 1600s
witnessed various attempts to claim legitimacy through history.
Magna Carta, for example, was cited by parliamentarians in 1628 as
proof that a monarch had recognised the liberties of Englishmen in
1215. However, this 'de tallagio non concendo' (confirmation of the
charter) was flawed. The Magna Carta had, in fact, secured the authority of the monarch over the barons as much as it embodied the rights of
every Englishman.

However, the civil wars that followed clearly had an impact as
writers sought explanations for their causes. County histories were
also written, evolving from a simple record of manorial and ecclesiastical antiquities to include new topics such as industry, agriculture,
geography and natural history. These, such as the works of John
Aubrey on Stonehenge and Avebury, laid the foundations of local
history and archaeology.

Seventeenth-century historians differentiated between memoirs and chronologies

There was growing awareness of the difference between annals, and
history. This was evident in Thomas Fuller's remark in *The Holy State*
(1642), that 'chronology, without history, is but a heap of tales'.
However, historians seemed intent – understandable given the tumul-
tuous events between 1642 and 1660 – to draw political lessons from
the past in a concise story that had a clear beginning and end. Here
are some examples:

▶ *Abel Boyer* – As journalist, Boyer maintained a record of the events of
Queen Anne's reign and added a commentary.

▶ *Gilbert Burnet's 'History of My Own Times'* – This book combined
autobiography and chronicle, but reflected on the role of the historian in the history of the Reformation. Burnet amassed documents,
and added an interpretation with a Protestant slant.

▶ *Clarendon's 'History of the Great Rebellion'* (1702-4) This book explained
  the causes of the civil war and gave a pro-royalist view, whilst vindi-
  cating Clarendon's own actions throughout the whole period. He
  made extensive use of documents, as did his enemies, to justify his
  arguments. Clarendon's emphasis on the ultimate positive outcome
  of the restoration, and the reign of Anne, set the style of later 'Whig'
  history in the eighteenth century which dwelt on England's progress
  and success.

The strong historical tradition outside Europe

China, Africa, the Middle East and India

It would be an error to only give an account of European historiography and to ignore the traditions of other parts of the world. For
example:

1. Chinese emperors, through several dynasties, regarded history as
    an important tool in teaching morality, truth and other educational
    values. Historians were attached to the imperial courts and
    chronicled their superior position in Chinese society.

2. In Africa, the ancient Egyptian histories were recorded in stone,
    emphasising military success, developments in religious beliefs, or
    political superiority.

3. Roman and Greek histories included accounts of the Egyptian and
    Carthaginian cultures.

4. The Middle East scholar, Ibn Khaldun (1332-1406) recorded his-
    tories of both his own region and those parts of Africa with which
    the Arabs had come into contact, usually by oral means. Khaldun
    sought to explain the differences between cultures and the workings
    of causation in history.

5. In India, a strongly established written tradition of Sanskrit and
    Persian texts kept a record of the south Asian past. Once again,
    there was an emphasis on promoting a political message and the le-
    gitimacy or benevolence of a dynasty.

Conclusion

The early historians were eager to use history to teach lessons about the present, and to guide future politics. In many cases they recorded what we would today call contemporary history. Oral sources were the most important. However, the Christian dependence on the Bible introduced a stronger reliance on written sources. By the Renaissance, scholars had begun to acquire written sources and combined these with classical models and the existing Christian tradition. In England's troubled seventeenth century, political lessons, or justifications, or a search for causes to explain the civil wars, compelled historians to cite written accounts as authorities. Elsewhere in the world, written records were well established and served to legitimatise the authority of the various dynasties.

Tutorial: helping you learn

Progress questions

1. What did Herodotus believe drove history?

2. Why did Polybius emphasise the political lessons of history?

3. What was Bede's purpose in his *Ecclesiastical History*?

4. In what sense was the Renaissance a 'rebirth' of an earlier historical method?

5. How was history written outside Europe?

Discussion points

1. Could one argue that the Renaissance made no new contribution to historical methods?

2. Why was the writing of history in Britain at the end of the seventeenth century still little more than a collection of annals?

Practical assignment
Make notes on this chapter using the following headings: Historical Methods, Strengths and Weaknesses. Write a short conclusion explaining the problems with historical writing that remained by around 1700.

Study and revision tips

1. Know the limitations of the early Classical historians, but do not judge them by the standards of modern historical writing of which they had no knowledge.

2. Note the importance of myth and religion to early history.

3. Rhetoric is a technique still used to persuade. It works by presenting two sides of an argument in an apparently impartial way, but then the presenter shows how one side is weaker than the other.

4. Notice how evidence was used to substantiate a viewpoint.

5. Observe how Renaissance scholars used history to suit their own political ambitions; this also still happens around the world.

3

The Ideas of Modern Historians

One-minute summary – From the Enlightenment of the eighteenth century to the late twentieth century, history has developed as a profession and subject. It has become characterised by certain methods and ideas. It has become more specialised, more rigorous, yet also more diverse. Certain schools of thought have emerged, and while supreme for a period, they have receded, become modified, or have been transcended by new ideas. Four strands seem particularly significant in this period: one, the growth of the Whig tradition and empiricism in British historical writing; two, the 'scientific' method of Leopold von Ranke; three, Karl Marx and the Marxist interpretation of history; and four, the Annales and 'total history'. However, outside Europe another influential school of history was that of Frederick Jackson Turner in the United States. In this chapter you will learn about:

▶ the Enlightenment and secular theories of causation
▶ Edward Gibbon's method and style
▶ Leopold von Ranke as the 'father of modern history'
▶ The Whig view of history in nineteenth-century Britain
▶ Karl Marx's new interpretation of history
▶ the Annales theory of 'a history of everything'
▶ historical writing outside Europe.

The Enlightenment and secular theories of causation

After the destructive religious wars of the seventeenth century, intellectuals in Europe turned to new explanations of the universe through scientific observation. New ideas spread quickly, thanks to increasing literacy amongst the wealthy, secular population and as a result of the development of printing. The Enlightenment was the name given to the criticism of the established religions, and the expression of ideas

which purported to be based on reason. The titles given to the intellectuals in the so-called 'Age of Reason' are:

1.   philosophes (French)
2.   Aufklärer (German)

Voltaire, Diderot and D'Alembert argued that society should be based on
human understanding, not religion, and that one had to comprehend the
laws that governed human nature. Nevertheless, philosophes did not
simply wish to debate, they wanted to change society; its educational
and legal systems, and above all, the political and administrative systems.
However, Jean Jacques Rousseau did not share the optimism of some
philosophes. He remarked: 'Man was born free, and everywhere he is in
chains.' He believed that 'progress' was not guaranteed. Whilst there was
virtue in man, man could not automatically create a virtuous society. He
felt that some form of organised religion was essential. Yet, overall, he also
subscribed to the idea that society should be based on reason.

Enlightenment histories were designed to teach 'civilisation'

Enlightenment *philosophes* aimed to use history as evidence of the way in
which the laws of human behaviour functioned. They wanted to show
that the Christian world view was flawed; they deliberately ignored
the virtue of Christians in the past, in order to illuminate the virtue of
other men. They also wanted to judge the past. They rejected the
method of collecting dates and events, or of relating only the principal
achievements of political and military leaders. They wanted to write
about the development of civilisation. This meant they could write
about genteel manners, customs, legal matters and political administration. By identifying the best features of human progress, they could
instruct others in how to construct a civilised society. In fact, their
works were designed for a specific audience; the emergent middle
classes and new rich of the eighteenth century.

Edward Gibbon's method and style

Gibbon combined a new accuracy and an engaging style

Edward Gibbon (1737-94) reflected the new Enlightenment approach,
but he also developed a distinctive style of his own. He was critical of
clerics and theologians, and of corruption and decadence. He felt that
emperors who succumbed to superstitions and vices were doomed.

His most famous work, *The History of the Decline and Fall of the Roman Empire* (published 1776-1788), suggested that great empires contained within them the seeds of their own demise. He appeared to celebrate the idea of civilisation. However, he did not condemn the historical tradition of the seventeenth century with its emphasis on facts and dates. He was critical of the philosophes who seemed content to praise administrative systems without reference to evidence. He pointed out errors made by other historians, whilst maintaining a mark of respect. He wrote: 'M. de Voltaire, unsupported by either fact or probability, has generously bestowed the Canary Islands on the Roman Empire'. (J. Warren, *History and the Historians*, p.51).

Gibbon's determination to achieve accuracy is evident in the use of footnotes. He was eager to show the precise origin of his evidence. He also wanted to avoid the philosophes' habit of inventing explanations, based on knowledge of human behaviour, where evidence did not exist. This honesty actually wins over the reader and leaves a satisfying sense of mystery which acts as an incentive to further study.

Gibbon's style more enduring than his historical method

Gibbon used irony to criticise his subject matter gently, and to expose individual historical figures as faintly ridiculous. This could be interpreted as an attempt to challenge, but also invite, the reader to look again at the subject matter. It would appear that Gibbon was encouraging his readers to make up their own minds. In fact, Gibbon's mocking actually conceals his persuasiveness. He was making the reader agree with him, without them always being aware of it.

One example of this was his use of two adjectives in the same sentence adjectives that carry entirely different meanings. Emperor Julian, for example, revived paganism, but his combination of 'severe manners of the soldier and philosopher were connected with some strict and frivolous rules of religious abstinence' (*Decline and Fall*, p. 352). 'Strict and frivolous rules', and 'severe', are used in juxtaposition to some previously praiseworthy comments on Julian. The reader is encouraged to feel that, despite his virtues, his religious concerns were a waste of time.

Gibbon's method contained weaknesses

Gibbon has been criticised for failing to offer a full explanation of causation in history. In *Decline and Fall*, he seemed to have created a narrative instead of an analysis of why the Roman Empire collapsed. However, Gibbon's introduction to *General Observations on the Fall of the*

Roman Empire in the West shows that he was surprised – given the weaknesses of the empire – that 'it subsisted for so long'. He argued that the 'deluge of barbarians', Christianity, and the 'loss of vigour' explained the decline of the empire, but conversely, that Christianity 'broke the violence of the fall'. Therefore, it is not Gibbon's causation that is at fault; he was able to show that history cannot be reduced to simple formulaic explanations. In this, he was far in advance of his philosophe contemporaries.

Where Gibbon can be criticised is in his eagerness to praise the institutions which he favoured. His condemnation of clericalism, and his praise for the 'mixed constitution' (which reflected his appreciation of English constitutional monarchy) arguably denied his work the accolade of a balanced history. It reflected his own prejudices, and his skilful style cannot conceal this simple fact.

Gibbon's contribution to historical writing was more than his style

Gibbon, like many of his contemporaries, still had no systematic method for analysing documentary sources. Gibbon could question their contents (providing the sources were already published), and comment on them, but he did not establish their author's purpose or the reliability and typicality of such sources. Rarely did he make comparative comments using other documents. He did try to use other sources, in contrast to other historians of the period, and he analysed coins, architecture and medals. He was not trained in palaeography and could not draw on many original sources. Perhaps the main drawback for Gibbon was that his style was personal. By addressing the reader, his work is accessible, but cannot claim to be impartial. Unkindly, we might say that Gibbon's style was closer to the novelist than the historian. However, there can be little doubt that the scale of Gibbon's work, and his engaging approach, was ahead of its time.

Leopold von Ranke as the 'father of modern history'

Leopold von Ranke (1795-1886) overturned the tendency to generalisation in history in favour of history 'wie es eigentlich gewesen ist' (history as it actually happened), that is, a rigorous analysis of original sources. He strived for objectivity instead of partiality, and established seminars as a forum for discussing historical issues as well as training historians. He has been criticised for laying emphasis solely on diplomatic and political history, and for considering only his own Prussian, conservative point of view. However, Ranke left a lasting legacy and many subsequent historians, although developing theories of their own, would have to acknowledge Ranke as the foundation of their profession, or even as the point of origin of their ideas.

The Enlightenment and contemporary events influenced Ranke's view of history

Ranke rejected the Enlightenment concepts that history could be explained in secular, rational terms, and that the study of systems would lead to progress in civilisation. He had studied theology, but he did not accept the rationalist explanation of faith at his university in Leipzig. Nor did he accept that God's presence in the world could be simply detected, and explained. Instead, he suspected that history could offer glimpses of the 'divine idea', and 'moments' when God intervened to influence the world's events.

Given that Ranke lived in a period when Europe was still recovering from the ravages of the Napoleonic Wars, and when German states were still coming to terms with the French occupation under Bonaparte, it is not surprising that he sought some explanation for these momentous trials. He was fascinated by the relationship between the human mind, the achievements of man and God's purpose for mankind. He could not accept that there was a simplistic explanation. German Enlightenment thinkers (*Aufklärer*) had accepted that God was still a factor in the world, unlike the French *philosophes*, so Ranke can be better understood in this context.

Ranke believed each epoch had a unique Zeitgeist (spirit of the age)

Ranke agreed with the German philosopher Herder that, far from entering an age of universal movements as the Enlightenment *philosophes* had advocated (where mankind would be united through rationality and science), Europe was seeing the flourishing of separate national identities. This led Ranke to believe that periods of history were marked by different ways of thinking. He advocated the study of the past epochs which acknowledged that values were different, and that they should be studied on their own terms. This was known as 'historicism', although it should be pointed out that this term now has different meanings.

Ranke's revolutionary ideas and methods

Ranke rejected the idea that history should be used to teach lessons. He wanted to recover the past for its own sake. He aimed to present the evidence, without making judgements based on contemporary values, so that the intentions of God, when he intervened, could be revealed. Ranke intended to let the past 'speak for itself' using the original sources as the mouthpiece. The doubts, hesitations and feelings of the authors of these documents could also be revealed, making the history more vivid and immediate. 'Wie es eigentlich gewesen ist' has been translated as 'how it actually happened', but it could also mean 'how it essentially happened'. This was, in short, how Ranke presented history. Yet he also imparted the methods of documentary analysis, and the training of the historian, which have made him famous.

Why Ranke has been criticised

Ranke has been criticised by some commentators for favouring his native Prussia, but this is misleading. As a Saxon, he was less enthusiastic about the state which had absorbed his homeland in 1815. It was the relationship of politics, nations, states and people which he found fascinating. Any historian could be forgiven for this, since most of them start by tackling the areas which most interest them.

In his *History of the Popes* (1834), Ranke maintained his discipline of objectivity despite his own Protestant leanings. Nevertheless, he was denied access to crucial archives, such as those of the Vatican, which would have greatly affected his work. His enthusiasm in discovering the papers of the Venetian elite, the Relazioni, according to Gino Benzoni (in Georg Iggers, ed., *Leopold von Ranke*, 1990), affected his judgement since he tended to overlook the style and deceptions of the authors. However, such errors have to be weighed against the accuracy achieved, and the impressive detail he commanded. Nor were his works narrowly focused, but broad and ambitious in scope, delivered with literary style.

It is unfair to criticise Ranke for only concentrating on political and diplomatic history, since he had to focus on events of significance. He could not hope to cover everything, and, in own words, he had to 'pay the greater attention to those [events] of world-historical importance' (*Civil Wars and Monarchy in France*, 1852).

The Rankean tradition was an influential legacy

After Ranke, historians tended to simplify or distort Ranke's views to suit their own interpretations and methods. Ranke was used to show that history was 'scientific' in its approach. It was confidently felt that objectivity was achievable, if hard work. Professorships of history were created in the new 'professional' climate. However, German historians glossed over Ranke's hesitations about the unification of their country in 1871. Neo-Rankeans tried to argue that Ranke's analysis of the growth of nations gave Germany a special status and they believed that the country's imperial expansion at the end of the nineteenth century was justified. Practically the only aspect of Ranke's ideas they didn't change was the method of documentary analysis. In Britain, there was already a tradition of historical writing that focused on the political constitution, but the Rankean method was used to reinforce it still further.

The Whig view of history

Whig history in Britain was dominant in the nineteenth century

The political settlement between William III and parliament in 1688 brought a pragmatic conclusion to the religious conflicts of the seventeenth century. English historians tended to interpret the past as a preparation for, or legacy of, this achievement.

The agricultural and industrial revolutions brought new wealth to Britain. England's military and naval victories secured a 'united kingdom' and then carved out a world empire. It is easy to understand the deep sense of optimism and self confidence about the past and the future. Whig history, named after the political party that had made the settlement with the crown in 1688, thus placed an enormous emphasis on 'progress'. By the mid-nineteenth century, Britain was the largest imperial power of the world and the leading industrial nation. Thomas Macaulay (1800-59), and Macaulay Trevelyan (1876-1962), praised England's intellectual and moral achievements. For Thomas Macaulay, each episode of *The History of England* was used to show how tyranny had been tamed, and progress made towards constitutional monarchy.

The Whig approach was challenged

Macaulay used literary devices to persuade the reader of his view. Take for example the case of Titus Oates, an alarmist who probably invented the 'Popish Plot' in 1678 to discredit Catholics during the reign of

Charles II. He was caricatured and ridiculed as an enemy of progress. Macaulay used the term 'we' to convince his readers of the right way to judge an historical episode. He aimed to popularise history, but also to instruct on the superiority of Englishmen's liberty. However, it was a moderate and sober liberty, vastly different from the excesses of the French revolution. The sense of achievement English readers enjoyed in Macaulay's, and then Trevelyan's work, reinforced the appeal of Whig history.

Not until after the First World War (1914-18) was this challenged. The enormous casualties of the war and the economic hardships of the 1920s and 1930s seemed to contradict the idea that England was 'progressing'. Herbert Butterfield *(The Whig Interpretation of History*, 1931) argued that the sweeping judgements of the Whig historians, or 'abridgements', had distorted truth. Their preference for using the past for 'present-minded' lessons was misleading.

As a result of Butterfield's criticism, a strong reaction arose against broad judgements and broad histories. Scholars burrowed more deeply into specialisms; history became more technical and more concerned with the past, not the present. Ironically, Butterfield shared the religious convictions of Ranke, but he helped to drive British historians away from the wide scope of Ranke's analysis into 'empiricism' (scholarship based strongly on evidence). This tradition has survived in the writing of PhDs even today.

Karl Marx's new interpretation of history

Karl Marx examined the economic causation of history

Karl Marx (1818-83) was not, strictly speaking, a historian. However, his interpretation of history, and his confident judgements on the future, were immensely influential. Marx rejected the assumption that history was driven by political élites, by nation states, or by God. He firmly believed that history was a succession of struggles between classes. These classes were the superstructures over the prevailing economic mode of production.

In his capitalist age, Marx used the work of Frederick Engels, who observed how the masses of urban industrial workers were alienated from their work by harsh conditions. Marx was appalled that the motive of capitalist entrepreneurs was profit, and that they were prepared to exploit the workforce for money. The workers themselves were forced to sell their labour in order to survive, but the system was inherently unfair; the competitive nature of capitalism demanded ruthless productivity which tended to force down wages, leaving the workers impoverished. Marx predicted that workers and employers would inevitably clash over the opposing interests. Eventually, Marx thought, the workers would prevail and overthrow the capitalist system by revolution.

Marxian ideas developed throughout his career
Marxian ideas, as opposed to the Marxist ideas of his successors, were developed and refined during his lifetime. It is therefore misleading to argue that the *Communist Manifesto* (1848) was the definitive version of his ideas. In fact, Marx's ideas have to be traced from across his career.

His view that the urban workers of Germany would rise up and overthrow the authorities was modified after the failure of the 1848 revolutions. Marx looked again at the unity of the classes in the newspaper serial *The Eighteenth Brumaire of Louis Napoleon* (1851). He discovered that the middle classes were bitterly divided by parties and economic interests, and that the working classes could be divided, or bribed, by unscrupulous dictators like Louis Napoleon (later Napoleon III).

Marx himself was an exile, which made it easier for him to reject the ideas of nationalism, but he did not escape the prejudices he held on other matters. He regarded the European peasantry as a 'doomed' class who belonged to a medieval epoch, and who were useless beyond service in the armies of authoritarians. He viewed the middle classes – the bourgeoisie – with loathing. He reserved the greatest venom for workers who seemed to work for the forces of reaction. He advocated a violent solution for the world he inhabited, and his prophecies bordered on arrogance.

The meaning of Marxian history
Marx presented a new view of history. Essentially it served a political purpose; it verified his theories and provided legitimacy for action in the future. Marx also offered an explanation of causation:

1. Economic forces could be identified as dominating each epoch, and these determined the social structure of each period. This was known as historical materialism.

2. Social tensions, or class struggle, led to revolutions where the pre-
    vailing economic system was overthrown. The inherent contradic-
    tions of the new system (a 'dialectic') would eventually set off a
    new class struggle, until that in turn was overthrown by revolution.

3. Only when the revolution of the proletariat (urban, industrial work-
    ers who were 'class conscious', or fully aware of their predicament)
    took place, and private property was abolished, would this process
    come to an end. With this would come the end of history since it
    would no longer be of any use.

Marx had therefore given history a model of change via economic development. Since the economic factor was the most important, this
was labelled 'economic determinism'.

Criticisms of Marxian history

As with all models, reality has a tendency to discredit them. By placing
all emphasis on economic determinism, Marx tended to discount other
factors which influenced the course of events. Under the Marxian
model all institutions and beliefs were determined by economic forces
– adminstrations, political systems, religious bodies, legal frameworks,
even systems of belief.

However, Marx ignored, either wittingly or unwittingly, the persuasive power of nationalism, and of organised religion. He tried to argue
that economic systems had dominated previous ages, but it would be
difficult to sustain an argument that the religious conflicts of the seventeenth century in Europe were purely economically determined.

Marx was also dismissive of economic systems he felt to be anachronistic. He condemned the 'Asiatic mode of production' in India as
stagnant, due to be replaced by the capitalism of the west. Marx also
spent a great deal of time defining classes, and analysing political movements, in order to interpret them using the model he had constructed.
In doing so, he relegated the importance of the factors in history.
However, his aim was to present to the world a coherent theory of revolutionary significance, not history for its own sake.

The legacy of Marxian analysis

In 1890 Frederick Engels tried to argue that he and Marx had not been
economic determinists, but he was forced to acknowledge that an economic force 'finally asserts itself as necessary'. In the *Eighteenth Brumaire*,

Marx was not able to make use of determinism per se because he was writing about contemporary events. But he still felt compelled to explain the divisions amongst the middle classes as dependent on 'their material conditions of existence', and he returned to this idea when citing historical examples in his work.

Marxists imposed the same model on history with great ruthlessness. All history in the Soviet Union, for example, had to conform to the Marxist model of rigid economic determinism. Certain periods of history were regarded as worthy of study simply because they fulfilled an ideological need. History was made to serve an oppressive world view. Argument, except on the refinement of the model's application to a period of history, was unknown. Evidence of the people's role, and the heroism of certain party icons, were all the evidence required.

British Marxists tried to restore the role of the individual's free will

After the Second World War (1939-45), British Marxists formed the Communist Party's Historian's Group in order to further their ideas and promote the communist interpretation of history. This seemed key, since it appeared that capitalism had produced the fascism of Hitler's Third Reich, and that Russia – the only Soviet country – had defeated it. However, the Soviet Union's repression of the Hungarians in the 1956 rising split the communist party in Britain and with it the historian's group. Christopher Hill, who had written a straightforward Marxist interpretation of the English Civil War in 1940 (*The English Revolution 1640*), turned away from the party which seemed to have endorsed the very behaviour for which it had criticised the fascists.

However, Hill, and others who left, did not abandon their Marxist principles. Indeed, they seemed even more determined to show that the will of the people, and the agency of free will, had a part to play in shaping history. They seemed to move away from the mechanistic idea that everything in history was 'economically determined'.

Economic base and social superstructure still equated to economic determinism

Marx had stated that the economic aspects of history were dominant. His successors argued either that this meant economic factors were the only ones worth studying, or that in some cases the superstructures (that is, other factors in history such as culture, religion and politics) could influence the base (economics).

Christopher Hill gradually moved towards the second of these inter-

pretations during his career; in the *English Revolution* he was an economic determinist, by the time he wrote *The Intellectual Origins of the English
Revolution* (1965) he argued that people's ideas were not simply a reflection of economic needs. However, Hill did not accept that economic
factors were anything other than dominant. He maintained that a person's class was a position defined in relation to other classes, but still
dependent on the productive process.

E. P. Thompson: the importance of human agency in history

Thompson, too, had left the historian's group in 1956. He seemed even
keener than Hill to establish the role of human free will above the impersonal forces of economics. His famous book *The Making of the English
Working Class* (1963) argued that the working class – far from being
created by the industrial revolution – actually predated it. He believed
that many trades were doomed to extinction, and that the actions of the
Luddites (workers who opposed machinery and progress) seemed back-
ward and futile, but that they were still worth studying. This was an
important contribution to history. Thompson sought to re-establish the
value of the past, instead of being in thrall to an ideological agenda. Yet
he did not acknowledge why his subject matter, the workers, were faced
by hardships and the loss of their trades: the very forces of economics he
was trying to play down.

Hobsbawm addressed broad issues and the impact of economics

Eric Hobsbawm had not left the historian's group in 1956; he remained
a staunch communist throughout his career. He wrote a series of books
on the great revolutions of the nineteenth century (*The Age of Revolution*,
1962), on the impact of capitalism (*The Age of Capital*, 1975), and on imperialism (*The Age of Empire*, 1987). These works maintained the Marxist
line of economic determinism, but their value lies in their contribution
to the writing of history. Without the Marxian analysis, history may
have continued to pursue only the political and diplomatic past.
Hobsbawm, like the other Marxist historians, wanted to take account
of the forces of economics. The nineteenth century had witnessed a pro-
found change in economic activity. The industrial revolution gave the
Europeans and the Americans an enormous advantage in terms of
trade, wealth and military power over the rest of the world. These
things could not be explained by politics and diplomacy alone.

The Marxist legacy is controversial

Marx offered an interpretation of history that suggested the links between economics and social structures. He also insisted on a use for history: it had a political purpose. Marxist historians subsequently tried to understand the world's history through the model that Marx created.

However, not all economic historical writing is Marxist. Economic history was already emerging as a specialism in its own right. The skills required by economic historians are often different from those required by, say, social historians. Skill in handling advanced statistics is a clear example. Such analyses owe little to the crude, often violent political slogans of Marxism.

However, Marxist views did inspire a new interest in social history. Thompson's work is one example. Yet Thompson was concerned that other Marxists seemed only to be interested in those workers who had contributed to the success of the labour movement, like a version of Whig history. George Rudé's excellent studies of the crowd also seemed to be about the workers, but it could be argued that Rudé was really interested in revolutions and people's behaviour in them.

Studies only of radicals and revolutionaries are a distortion

One of the chief criticisms of Marxist historians is their desire to study only those aspects of history which reinforce their ideas. At worst, this can lead to the deliberate omission of evidence which contradicts a cherished theory. Christopher Hill rescued from obscurity the radical groups of the Cromwellian era in *The World Turned Upside Down* (1972), but in doing so he gave the impression that these groups had somehow been typical of the period, if not in the majority. Non-radical groups were played down, or ignored, because Hill's purpose was to draw our attention to the radicals. This reveals another problem for historians: the selection of evidence and examples.

Since the collapse of the Soviet system in Eastern Europe and Russia, Marxist ideas have been discredited. There is little sympathy for the ideological strait-jackets of the so-called meta-narrative (theoretical and universal interpretation). However, the phenomena that Marxists have drawn our attention to will not disappear. For example, there is still a need to understand the idea of 'revolution'.

1. Is it a '*re*volution', a returning cycle of events?
2. Is it a violent and abrupt change?

3. Is it an overthrow of one power by another?
4. Or are revolutions always characterised by the involvement of the masses?

The Annales theory of 'total history'

In France, before the First World War, there was some disquiet about the Rankean method. It appeared to emphasise the recovery of factual material solely through documents, and promoted the kind of nationalism and supremacist ideas which Germans had used to justify their assertiveness in European affairs between 1871 and 1914.

From the 1880s, a new approach to social science appeared in the form of sociology. This seemed to offer new possibilities to historians because it established theoretical models which could be used to make sense of social structures. In addition, human geography looked as if it could assist the historian, too. The distribution of settlements, demography, migration patterns, the influence of soils and climate on human activity – all seemed to suggest that an inter-disciplinary approach would yield a better understanding of the past.

March Bloch (1886-1944) was one of the first French historians to see the potential of this. He was dissatisfied with the Rankean emphasis on 'great events' and 'great men', and began to explore the possibilities of research into his local region, the Ile de France, using geography and fieldwork to assist him.

Bloch's new methods of analysis

Bloch's starting point was always a broad question, rather than a set of documents or an hypothesis. He did not set out to prove or disprove an idea, but to answer a question. His first interest was the medieval peasant of France. He observed how, in some parts of rural France, farming methods appeared to have changed very little. There was clear potential for research into the lives of peasants, and clues in the landscape to the medieval past. As he worked using this 'regressive method', he realised the great importance of the landscape in shaping the lives and techniques of the peasants.

However, Bloch did not limit himself to geography. He was interested in group psychology, too. In *Les Roi Thaumaturges* (*The Royal Touch*, 1924), he asked how the people could have believed that their monarchs had the power to heal through touch. He described a phenomenon of 'collective mentalities'.

Bloch's later works, *French Rural History* (1931) and *Feudal Society* (1939-40), expanded still further his command of other disciplines. He used archaeology, psychology, geography, literature, languages, the interpretation of place names, economics and cartography. *Feudal Society* covered the period 900-1300 AD, and the canvas of his subject matter is vast. It was labelled 'total history' since it appeared to try to cover almost every aspect of the past.

Bloch's methods can be criticised

Given the vast range of Bloch's work, there was a danger that significant details would be obscured. For example, *Feudal Society* gave only a brief sketch of the clergy, which, given their central role in the cultural and political shaping of rural France, was surely a major oversight. Despite his use of sociology, Bloch failed to achieve the accuracy that the subject's founder, August Comte, would have expected.

Sociologists claimed that by identifying the laws that governed human activity, they could construct accurate models, in the same way that science had identified laws in the universe. This concept was known as positivism. Bloch was also not exempt from imposing his values on the past. He tried to argue that rural France was nationalistic in a period when the concept of nationalism had not yet been realised. This confusion may well have been the product of Bloch's personal experiences, as he had served alongside soldiers from the countryside during the First World War. He also became a member of the French resistance in the Second World War, until captured and shot by the Nazis.

Lucien Febvre: the Annales

Febvre (1878-1956) established the Annales as the dominant genre in French academic institutions by his force of personality and argument. He said that the inter-disciplinary approach gave a more truthful picture of the past than the narrow political and militaristic approach of the Rankeans. He founded, with Bloch, the journal *Annales d'histoire économique et sociale* in 1929, which still flourishes today. Febvre continued Bloch's idea of using other disciplines in his work. His *Philippe II et la France-Compte* (1912) began with a focused question and relied heavily on geography. *The Problem of Unbelief in the Sixteenth Century: The Religion of Rabelais* (1942) combined geography with group psychology ('*outillage mental*').

Fernand Braudel: a new standard in writing total history

Braudel (1902-85) wrote his massive *The Mediterranean and the Mediterranean World in the Age of Philip II* (1949) whilst in a German prison camp. Its range is breath-taking. The first volume, and most of the second, establishes the geographical setting of the Mediterranean in exhaustive detail. Only towards the end of the entire work does normal 'history' appear. Braudel was deterred form covering the detail of Philip II's policies, the wars and the actions of the élites. Instead, one is left feeling that the powerful forces of nature dwarf the actions of the human protagonists.

This work gave the title 'La longue durée' (the long view or duration) to the Annales, suggesting that slow, almost imperceptible, changes were as important as the fast-moving political events of the élite few. Another title that Braudel bestowed on this idea was 'geo-history'. The attempt to explore all the possibilities of the question he posed was not limited by the artificial boundaries created by man, such as national borders, the reigns of monarchs, or the epochs which appear to begin and end with precision.

Criticisms of total history – the role of the individual?

It should be noted that the Annales scholars did not set out to write a 'history of everything'. Total history meant the attempt to answer a specific question in its totality, or as nearly as possible. However, Braudel really did not acknowledge the role of religion in his work (the collective mentality). By relegating the political changes of the period as much as he did, he gave the impression that individuals had very little impact at all on the great forces of nature. This seems hard to justify given the enormous power and authority some monarchs wielded. It seems equally hard to accept given the impact of the ideas of Martin Luther and Jean Calvin in the Reformation.

The Annales concentration on the medieval and early modern periods suited their approach, and the scarcity of documents. It would be hard indeed to create a total history of the late modern period, such as the nineteenth and twentieth centuries. Another criticism was that, in placing so much emphasis on the imperceptibility of change in the *longue durée*, it was difficult to account for change, and causation, at all.

The development of the Annales continued throughout the twentieth century

The Annales developed still further after Braudel's work had been published. One branch of the movement grew into quantitative history, partly due to the influence of the Marxist Ernest Labrousse. Pierre Chaunu also moved towards the quantative approach in his *Seville and the Atlantic*, where, in an emulation of Braudel's *Mediterranean*, he traced the largely economic trends of Atlantic trade within a geographical setting. Chaunu also tried to combine the history of short-term events ('conjuncture') with long-term trends ('structure').

Another part of the Annales developed the inter-disciplinary approach, but in a fascinating detail. The best known is the work of Emmanuel Le Roy Ladurie. *The Peasants of Languedoc* (1966) began with the Annales geo-historical setting, but Ladurie did not abandon the chronological approach and narrative. The best-loved of his works, though, was *Montaillou* (1975) which narrated the story of one village in France in the fourteenth century. The whole mentality of the peasants was explored in the Annales fashion, but the most popular section of the book contained direct quotations by the peasants, recorded by a Catholic church inquisitor searching for heretics. Ladurie had written a highly successful micro-history with the vividness that direct quotation offers.

The legacy of the Annales survives today

The exploration of mentalities, and the inter-disciplinary approach, has opened to the historian the tools of other subjects, and other fields of research. In contrast to the determinism of Marxism, the Annales opened new avenues of research, and new interpretations. The history of the body, for example, owed its existence to the combination of the Annales thinking, cultural anthropology and psychology.

Yet, curiously, the Annales concept itself has not taken root outside of France, with the exception perhaps of Poland. This may have been in part due to the technical language, the emphasis on detail, and the preponderance of geography over history. It may also have been due to the strong currents of historical styles that already existed in Britain, America and Germany. In addition, the determinism and lack of individual free will in shaping events has never been attractive in western historiography; the result of the liberal tradition of promoting the role and status of the individual. However, the 'New Histories', examining every aspect of the past rather than just the political, or event-based narrative, do owe their development to the Annales. History is a subject much richer for their contribution.

Historical writing outside Europe

Frederick Jackson Turner believed in 'manifest destiny'

In America during the nineteenth century, historians tried to make sense of the forces that had shaped, and were still shaping, the country. Immigration, growing urbanisation, and the expansion west in the vast hinterland were explained in the context of the dominant credos of Protestantism, nationalism and entrepreneurial spirit.

This whole range of ideas was encapsulated in the works of Frederick Jackson Turner (1861-1932). Turner wrote about the role of the frontier in American history – not as a political phenomenon, but as the factor that had shaped the entire culture of the American people. The inevitability of the progress of white settlers across the 'wilderness', the settlement of new communities, and the acquisition and development of land for agriculture all suggested that Americans had a 'manifest destiny' before them.

The optimism of this thesis, and its obvious supremacist and prophetic overtones, was popular in the United States, but Turner had also set the scene for the writing of a type of history that was not simply political, but social and economic too. In South America too, there was a feeling that their own history was unique and deserved to be written in a way that set them apart from Europeans. The liberation of the South American states from Spanish and Portuguese colonial rule offered a chance to create a national identity and a sense of direction, and history was harnessed to that end.

Conclusion

This chapter has dealt with some of the most influential movements of modern historical writing. The Enlightenment view of history developed out of a dissatisfaction with relying on metaphysical arguments (views that cannot be disproven, based on religion) to explain the motors of history. Edward Gibbon developed a style that was ironic but persuasive, reminding the historian that historical writing is partly a literary exercise. But the greatest change came with the work of Ranke who offered a model of causation, a method of research and a demand for the professionalisation of the subject. Ranke had an enormous impact on western historical writing. The emphasis on original sources and rigorous analysis has endured and survives in the way that most PhDs are completed.

In Britain the emphasis on evidence, or empiricism, also endured, but it was made more popular by the optimism of Whig histories with their emphasis on progress. Marx reinterpreted history from the point of view of economics, and the connection between economics and society, but again, it was the result of dissatisfaction with the world he lived in. Marx failed to offer a more comprehensive analysis of the past. He neglected the other factors which influence events, because he was a polemicist seeking to promote his theory of revolutionary change for the future. Those who subscribed to Marxian analysis were faced by the difficulty of the deterministic nature of economics in Marx's model of historical change. How important was free will? A similar dilemma had emerged with the Annales, who had sought to answer wide questions without limiting the scope of the evidence. Inevitability was a theme also enjoined by Turner in the USA; a deep sense of progress and achievement in the conquest of the west was used as an icon of the character of the people of the United States.

Tutorial: helping you learn

Progress questions

1. Why did the Philosophes want to emphasise 'reason' as causation in history?

2. Why did Ranke feel that the past should 'speak for itself'?

3. What was Whig history?

4. What is meant by 'historical materialism'?

5. What was the contribution of the Annales school to the writing of history?

Discussion points

1. Are there 'laws' of historical development (such as economic determinism) which are true?

2. Have 'laws' in history only served ideologies?

Practical assignment

Write a page to address the following quotation using this chapter:

'Science and reason bring progress; religion brings distortion and stagnation.' Is this true?

Study tips

1. Learn the aims of Ranke, Marx and the Annales as well as their methods.

2. Make a list of the ways in which each group thought that history had aspects which were inevitable.

3. If you are asked to write an essay about any of these movements, try to balance their positive contributions with your criticisms.

4. Note how the contemporary worlds and events in which the main historians of this chapter lived influenced their approach to history.

4

Current Issues in History

One-minute summary – In the 1960s in Britain, Whig history came under attack from Lewis Namier and E. H. Carr. Geoffrey Elton challenged Carr for assuming that facts could not 'speak for themselves'; he defended the rational, Rankean use of sources in history and the professionalism of the subject. However, in the 1970s a new challenge was mounted on history and historians. 'Post-modernist' thinkers rejected the idea that historians could be impartial, and attacked the way that historians wrote their texts. They argued that language itself was misleading: history was little more than a fiction too often used for dangerous and oppressive ends. Amongst the new, post-modernist histories that appeared was Edward Said's work on Orientalism. This attacked the way that western histories on the East had perpetuated the oppression of the peoples who lived there. Such was the impact of post-modernism that historians such as Keith Jenkins called for a complete overhaul of the discipline. However, Richard Evans has mounted a counter-attack, pointing out the real value of history and the advantages of absorbing the more positive aspects of the 'new histories'. In this chapter you will learn about:

▶ Namier and the attack on Whig history
▶ the views on factual history of Elton and Carr
▶ the post-modernist challenge to history
▶ how the New Histories emerged
▶ how history counter-attacked the post-modernists.

Namier and the attack on Whig history

Empiricism and progress: Namier's challenge to Whig history
Lewis Namier challenged the theoretical nature of history which he felt was common to both Whig history and the Marxist interpretation. He advocated instead an absolute reliance on archival research and painstaking care in documentary analysis.

Namier championed an idea called 'structural analysis'. In his book *The Structure of Politics at the Accession of George III* (1929), he avoided the usual examination of the development of the British parliament. Instead he used prospography – a collection of biographies – to show that parliament's actions were not governed by the actions of the Tory and Whig parties, but by individual MPs. He examined their self-interest, rivalry, and use of relations or contacts to further their ambitions. He also rescued the reputation of George III who had been seen as the enemy of democracy, even as a conspirator who had sought to acquire more personal power. Namier's publication of parts of his private papers reflected his interest in that type of source as the most honest, most revealing category of evidence available to the historian.

Namier tried to achieve objectivity

Nevertheless, Namier's obsession with the mind and thinking of the individual tended to obscure and override the part played by ideas in history. Namier placed much faith in the Freudian analysis of the human mind. In so doing, he fell victim to imposing the same laws of human nature in determining history that he had criticised in the Whigs and Marxists.

Equally Namier was criticised for only considering the individuality of the aristocracy – his own class, in fact. Although the masses were subject to the same psychoanalysis, they remained the impersonal mob. Namier has often been seen as successful in his efforts to be objective and impartial. His scholarship seemed to embody the Rankean tradition completely. However, Pieter Geyl (*Debates with Historians*, 1962) argued that complete impartiality rendered history pointless; it had to make comment on the past. Yet Geyl also warned against history's use as a tool of political ideologues, preferring to see history serving the cause of 'comprehension, open-mindedness ... [as] the very breath of civilisation'.

The views on 'factual history' of Elton and Carr

E. H. Carr argued (*What is History?*, 1961) that history was not an accumulation of facts and events; rather it was a subject shaped by the historians. Facts, he said, do not 'speak for themselves'. Consequently we needed to know something about the historian, what makes the historian 'tick'. Anticipating the challenge to this idea, Carr argued that, when facts are presented, they are scrutinised by other historians. If there is a general acceptance of the fact presented, it becomes a 'historical fact', but it is still reliant on the interpretation of the historian.

G. R. Elton disagreed. He argued in *The Practice of History* (1967) that there was no need for the interpretation to qualify any fact as an 'historical fact'. Elton insisted that history was about 'what happened'. If it was relegated to a set of interpretations, then accuracy would suffer, since all interpretations would have to be acknowledged as having some validity (this is known as relativism). Elton believed that some evidence was vague and required interpretation, and he pointed out that selection was also required to make sense of the evidence. The best form of defence against distortion, Elton maintained, was professional scholarship.

Carr fell into the trap of positivism

Carr's error was not so much pointing out that historians can influence, and distort, the evidence – the usual argument against him – but in believing that objectivity could be achieved through an understanding of development in history. Carr would probably have escaped serious criticism, had he not also insisted that historians should have an awareness of the likely shape of the *future*. This positivistic notion meant that Carr's version of history would include prediction and strongly suggested 'inevitability' in history.

This seems to be a trap to be avoided. Take the case of Paul Kennedy, a prolific historian on diplomacy who wrote *The Rise and Fall of the Great Powers: Economic Change and Military Conflict from 1500-2000* (1988). Kennedy predicted the relative decline of the USA in the 1990s, yet a year after publication it was the USSR that collapsed. Since the Cold War, the USA has taken up a new and dynamic role in world affairs – hardly the decline that Kennedy predicted.

Karl Popper and the use of history to oppose historicism

The question of relativism was touched upon in the 1950s by Karl Popper, a philosopher and social scientist. Popper criticised the concept of historicism in his book *The Poverty of Empiricism* (1957). Historicism can be defined in two ways:

1. One cannot understand the past without reference to present day ideas and values.

2. There are laws or historical processes that undermine human free will.

In other words, Popper disliked the idea of all-encompassing theories to explain the world – Marxism, for example. He felt that history itself was influenced by the growth of knowledge, and this could not be predicted. Far from being able to identify 'deterministic' processes like class struggle, to predict the future, Popper identified a 'methodological individualism', which made prediction impossible. Furthermore, attempts to build laws of historical development were but a thin disguise for totalitarian ideologies; 'inevitability' was a way they condemned their opponents. Popper wanted history to be used to educate people in order to avoid such ideas.

The post-modernist challenge to history

The definition of post-modernism
Post-modernism is a disparate set of theories which emerged as an attack on established modes of thinking during the 1970s. It developed from three roots within western culture: art, architecture, and literary criticism.

1. In art and architecture, post-modernism was a radical and alternative way of looking at the world. It sought to turn existing ideas on their head using humour and irony, or shock tactics.

2. In literary criticism, new analyses of texts revealed that words had great power, a power that could be wielded by authors with great effect. Moreover, it was alleged that academics – as authors – deliberately misled their readers with claims that they could establish rational, true views of the world. Historians thus became the object of attack.

Saussure on the power of language
Ferdinand de Saussure (1857-1913) had written that words convey different meanings in different languages, and that these differences could matter. Language had a set of rules, or structure, which had to be strictly obeyed in order to create meaning.

Post-structuralists, more recently, argued that language is the only means we have to establish what is real. However, there was much doubt whether the so-called rational claims of academics and scientists, to establish what is real, were valid. Far from being able to identify and explain reality, the post-structuralists claimed, we could do neither. Moreover, our very language was misleading.

However attractive these premises appear to be, they have really done more harm than good. For example, is it untrue to say that language is all that we have to establish what is real? What about the power of thought, or the deduction of logic? Post-structuralists maintain that it is not possible to identify or explain what is real, yet they ignore the absurdity of their own denial. If a historian identifies and explains an event, post-structuralists would not only deny that is what she or he is doing, but that neither the event, nor the explanation, is real!

Derrida and the deconstruction of texts

Jacques Derrida used a technique called 'deconstruction' to interpret texts. He argued that it was not simply the words that had power, but the symbols and signs that those words, gaps and omissions conjured. Derrida then jumped to the conclusion that the author is not in control of the language, but none of these signs follow a rational pattern. In this sense, he said, one could argue that the author was absent from the text. Historical texts were simply examples of rhetoric, or the results of other texts (this is called inter-textuality). But Derrida also exposed his real motive when he pointed out that texts simply reflect the prevailing culture, which, in the West, was riddled with ethnocentrism (a form of racism) and colonial attitudes. His charge then, was that western historical writing was essentially tyrannical.

Foucault, White and the use of power

Michel Foucault believed that language communicated power. Opposition to that power was labelled at best untrue, or at worst the products of the insane. His books reflect his scepticism about history, and his interest in power and psychology. An example was his history of the organisations of prisons in *Discipline and Punish* (1977). Curiously, in explaining that he had written a history, Foucault admitted that he had 'never written anything but fictions'. Perhaps this invites us to ignore him, since he is anything but a historian. Or should we accept his honesty?

Hayden White (*Metahistory*, 1973) accepted that some evidence could be established as real. However, the historian who used the evidence to shape a history imposed his or her own view on them. This was a return to Carr in one respect, but White was concerned at how historians seemed to weave together a text for their own purposes, an emplotment, just like a fictional story. This process was called a meta-narrative. This view contrasts completely with Derrida's 'absent' author.

A response to White and the prejudice of the author
It is interesting that, from Carr through to the post-modernists, the role of historians has been seen as somehow negative. Their influence is shown as a distortion, or worse still as an exercise in power. Yet these word games by post-modernists reveal that it is they that have the obsession with power, not the historian. The historian freely admits that discussion and interpretation are crucial to the subject. No historian would claim to know all history, to have the only true interpretation. It is through the acceptance, rejection and modification of opinion and interpretation that historians hope, collectively, to reveal a fuller picture of the past. The discovery of new evidence, and the development of new ideas, both contribute towards this process.

The weaknesses of post-modernist history were more than philosophical

Post-modernism began as a rejection of modern beliefs that we can know 'truth' and 'reality'. Post-modernists denied that science could ensure progress and civilisation. They pointed to the carnage of world wars, the invention of nuclear weapons, the spread of industrial pollution, and the rape of the environment. They expressed great anger at the complacency of western academic institutions.

The post-modernists thought that they had found the explanation for the imperialism of western nations in the nineteenth and twentieth centuries, rooted in the culture, and lying in the texts for all to see. They criticised what they saw as the creation of meta-narratives or ideologies through language, perpetuated through the insistence that academics cite each other in their sources.

However, the post-modernists are surely guilty of the very things they criticise. They have constructed their own ideologies; they have sought and imposed an explanation of the past using their own contemporary values. They have accused others of misleading us, and yet by their own definition have no way of establishing that their own ideas are true. Indeed, their ideas might be false. Have they not succeeded only in confirming their own negation?

Said's Orientalism offered a new view of colonialism

Edward Said's ground-breaking book *Orientalism* (1978) is a case example of post-modernist history, but also a link to the development of the so-called New Histories. Said examined the theory of imperialism within the texts of contemporary sources (called discourses). He discovered that imperialists developed a system of knowledge, and hence power, over the peoples of the Orient. His book was not about the Orient itself. Rather, it was about how the British and French had constructed a pervasive view of the Orient that actually influenced imperialist policies and even how Oriental people viewed themselves. The Orientals, known as the 'Other' were stigmatised as the imperialists' 'problem'.

This view was perpetuated by western academic writing, and turned into a taxonomy (an example so accepted that it was thought to be true). However, Said has been heavily criticised. The idea that he is somehow exempt from the knowledge-power relationship, in order to make judgements of his own on the past, is ignored. Said defended his analysis as being based on the 'human spirit', but in fact the basis of his approach was the same western liberal tradition he was attacking. There seems to be an inconsistency too in how this relationship of power can be changed. Despite the attack on meta-narratives, there seems to be little or no acknowledgement of the part played by individuals in history.

How the New Histories emerged

The New Histories: women

It would be wrong to attribute the emergence of new histories solely to the effect of post-modernism. The works of Marx and EP Thompson had their own legacies in terms of promoting the study of socio-economic history. The Rankean emphasis on politics and diplomacy acknowledged the importance of cultural history, too.

However, new specialisms have developed in relatively recent years.

▶ *Example* – Women's history first emerged as a genre that sought to redress the balance of writing by examining the role that women had played in the past. Moving from the exceptional individuals, to the experience of the mass majority of women, was achieved relatively rapidly, but the development of women's histories, to embrace the context and inter-connections of the woman's experience through time, has been slower. Even today, there remains a strong emphasis on attacking the patriarchy of society, rather than the integration of women's history with other aspects of the discipline.

New specialisms have developed from gender history, through the history of medicine to the many aspects of cultural history.

The New Histories: local history

Local history has grown in popularity in recent decades and has played an increasingly important role in 'mainstream' history. The geographical location of archives in Britain, based in provincial towns and cities, have made them accessible to a large number of historians, both amateur and professional.

Local history has remained largely in the Rankean tradition, and it is easy to understand why. The type of sources available require considerable scholarly examination, and sometimes a command of specialist knowledge. Field and settlement names, for example, require a firm grasp of agricultural history, possibly Latin or other old English and Saxon words, an awareness of geography, and a detailed knowledge of the changes wrought on the landscape. Local history has already revealed new information on demographic changes to Britain; these include the effects of urbanisation and industrialisation, the impact of the agricultural revolution, the dramatic consequences of diseases and the changes in family size and structure. Many of these findings are the result of years of meticulous research and quantative analysis, not unlike an army of Annales historians.

How history counter-attacked the post-modernists

New directions: globalisation

Before analysing the position today, and offering a conclusion on modern historical writing, we need to be aware of the emerging trend towards globalisation and comparative history. Faced with an increasing mass of information, partly fuelled by the computer revolution, there is both a need for knowledge to be delivered clearly and effectively, and a need for it to be clearly demarcated from 'information'.

Faced with a 'critical mass' of data, some have predicted that the new 'information age' will bring about the death of the monograph. Such gloomy predictions have been made before, but the likelihood of the screen replacing the page as a medium for gaining substantial quantities of knowledge seems slim.

Probably there will be a greater demand for:

1. histories which encompass the global, or at least the world-regional, perspective

2. studies that combine political, social, economic, cultural, military, literary and many other specialisms in the subject.

History continued to serve the creation of national identities at the turn of the twenty-first century. For example, in South Africa, and in the former Soviet Republics, the achievements of the people and their leaders are strongly expressed. However, it seems equally certain that there will continue to be a demand for the specialisms of history in their own right, which is a positive testament to the interest that history continues to generate.

Conclusion

Richard Evans (*In Defence of History*, 1998) traced how the crisis in history, caused by the post-modernist challenge, developed. He argued that historians could still reach 'genuine insights' into past events. He rejected the word-play of post modernists, but accepted their charge that language has had a powerful influence in the writing of history.

Nevertheless, historians have long been aware of the role played by interpretation and opinion; this is part of the process of historical debate. Discussion and the sharing of ideas, through conferences, papers, journal articles and books, and increasingly through electronic means, enable historians to create a picture of the past which is more honest than the view of a single person. To simply condemn all historians as tyrants, imperialists, or worse, is meaningless and destructive. Worse still, the idea that all interpretations have equal validity, without any reference to academic rigour, would mean that those who claim that the Holocaust did not happen are equally truthful. This reaches a level of grotesque absurdity; it is surely a dangerous and immoral position to deny that millions perished in the Nazi death camps.

Tutorial: helping you learn

Progress questions

1. What was Carr's criticism of history as it was practised in Britain in the 1950s?

2. What did Derrida and Foucault share in their views of how texts, and consequently how history, was written?

3. What are the New Histories?

4. How have historians, like Richard Evans, responded to post-modernism?

Discussion points

1. 'Post-modernism applied to the study and writing of history is a dangerous drug; and, like a dangerous drug, it must be avoided at all costs.' Do you agree?

2. What were the motives behind post-modernism? Did this affect the way they approached history, and if so, was this any different from previous historical thinkers?

3. What implications might this have for future historical writing?

4. Can it be determined, if there had been no previous established method of writing history, how historians should approach history?

Practical assignment

Write a side of paper on how, in the light of the methods described so far in this book, you would prefer to see history written. Justify your method.

Study and revision tips

1. Try to understand the post-modernist challenge rather than simply rejecting it.

2. Look at the effectiveness of the historians' defence; make a note of their main points.

3. Note how histories that used post-modernism have sometimes enriched the subject.

4. Make a list of the concepts listed in this chapter and their meanings. The vocabulary of the post-modernists is specific, but often overused.

5

A Historical Method

One-minute summary – To clarify where history now stands, and what the prevailing methods are, this chapter will show the approach and the outline of some key methods that are used. Despite the challenge that historians cannot be objective – as if that were some sort of crime – some subjective comment might be useful. Interpretation enriches the subject; shared interpretation, which avoids inaccuracy, can be of enormous benefit. The post-modernists focused on individual texts and their flaws, but failed to appreciate the balance that could be achieved collectively. After all, the historian does not write for himself or herself, but for others. Historians are engaged in solving problems, such as causation and consequence, similarity and difference, and weighing the relative importance of events and people. Other disciplines have given historians an array of tools to use. Combined with their own determination, questioning, challenging, detective work, and reflection, historians are better equipped now than ever before. In this chapter you will learn about:

▶ approaching history philosophically
▶ the types of history and comparative history
▶ approaching history in a practical way.

Approaching history philosophically

The earliest historians believed that history had contemporary value

Classical historians had tried to use history to teach lessons for the benefit of the present generation. In some cases, they aimed to 'put the record straight'. There were attempts to explain the cause of events, too. From the end of the Roman period through to the Renaissance, there were problems with the selection of past events, in that they tended to produce long lists of chronology. However, history continued to be used to promote ideologies, and to teach moral or political lessons into the eighteenth century.

Modern historical writing has diversified

In Britain the empirical tradition took root, focusing on the analysis of original sources. On the continent of Europe, Leopold von Ranke's methodology emphasised political and diplomatic history, and the analysis of documentary sources.

Marx and the Annales initiated new directions in the study of history: the importance of geography, economics, social conditions, and the 'long view' of change. They stressed the importance of impersonal forces, rather than the actions of individuals. But these apparently determinist approaches were rejected by many academics, such as Karl Popper and Lewis Namier. The role of human agency seemed too great a factor to be lost sight of.

However, the profession was soon debating whether it was possible to be objective and impartial, and even whether that was desirable. Style, interpretation, opinion, the prevailing influences of the period in which the history was written and the historians background – all seemed to suggest that historians could not be objective. Post-modernists went further, and argued that all texts were fictions: the past was irrecoverable, and only the historian's opinion was 'real'. This attack did not prevent the emergence of more histories. In fact, history has diversified and flourished. Today, accounts of a single household stand alongside histories of the body, of culture, of literature, and so on.

Objectivity – a goal for historians

Objectivity is a discipline. It is the means of suppressing a historian's tendency to judge on the basis of his or her own values.

▶ *Example* – It would be slightly ridiculous to argue that Charles I should have averted the English Civil War by setting up the kind of parliamentary democracy which Britain has now. This would be a form of relativism. It is more important to try to understand, and present, the ways of thinking of the period. Hence, in this example, we would need to explain Charles' aspirations, and his options, within the belief system of the time. By doing this, we gain an understanding of Charles, his time, and avoid the pitfalls of value-judgements (judging the past by our own standards).

With contentious issues of the past, objectivity allows us to present to present all sides of the argument. Where the issue is still controversial today, the objective historian will present the views of both contemporaries, and historians, who disagree.

Subjectivity can have value

Historians need to acknowledge that the people of the past held subjective viewpoints. The existence of such viewpoints is itself a fact. By citing the views of the past, in direct quotations for example, the history presented is more vivid, and 'real'.

▶ *Example* – An excellent example of this is the work of Lyn Macdonald. Macdonald's histories of the First World War include hundreds of first-hand accounts by soldiers and civilians caught up in the conflict. The quotations are linked by a narrative of events, and an explanation of the background to each of the comments.

Historians' comments not only make sense of the events, but make history interesting.

Style, based on command of language, is what made Edward Gibbon's work so popular. Popularity means that historical work is accessible by a wide audience. History need not be 'as dry as dust'. Our subject matter – the past – has been informative and entertaining, too. Comments by the historian, the subjective element, are not necessarily negative anyway. They remind us that history is diverse, rich, contentious, and challenging. Diversity makes the world more fascinating, and a history that reflects diversity is truer to the real world.

What is not acceptable, however, is inaccuracy. It is reasonable to form a judgement so long as that judgement can be supported with evidence. Inaccuracy, distortion, and the deliberate selection of atypical evidence are the result of inadequate rigour.

Significance is an important element in the selection of evidence

Where there is a mass of data, it is easy to become overwhelmed, and then fail to pick out the key feature of a study. The way to avoid this is to establish a question, and then select material against it.

▶ *Example* – If a historian were trying to establish the causes of the South African War (1899-1902), detailed studies of the lives of South Africans in agricultural communities in 1898, whilst fascinating, would not address the particular question. What could be of significance would be the lives of those South Africans who had grievances with the British. In other words, some process of selection would need to take place. This selection, of course, will depend on the subject matter. A study into agricultural change in South Africa during the late nineteenth century would need to incorporate details of the farmers' lives. It is not easy to pick out the significant aspects of a subject from the mass of detail, and some subjectivity is usually acknowledged.

Determinism and human agency are still debated

Determinism is not generally popular with historians. It implies an inevitability about events, and immutable laws that govern human nature. This form of positivism has been more popular among sociologists and psychologists seeking models of social structure and behaviour.

Given the diversity of history, and the adoption of a more interdisciplinary approach, it might seem necessary to incorporate these social-scientific models. However, they remain only models, and historians often point out that reality in the past never followed any 'model' path.

(a) Nevertheless, historians need to acknowledge that long-term trends, and impersonal forces, do exert influences on individuals and societies.

(b) Equally, the remarkable story of mankind has been punctuated by exceptional individual achievement, often seemingly against the odds.

Both long-term and impersonal, and short-term and individual factors are important. Historians are often fascinated by change, and by continuity, and trying to understand and explain what drives them.

Causation fascinates historians

The Annales school of history reminds historians that there is seldom a single cause of historical events. Even Marx admitted (in *Eighteenth Brumaire*) that his model of socio-economic causation could be interrupted by political events. Historians often disagree about the relative importance of factors which caused an event. This generates debate which, as already explained, is a beneficial by-product of the profession. Cause, and consequence, remain popular topics for historians.

Understanding is the key to the historian's work

One of the primary motivations for historians remains the desire to understand the past. No longer are they content to narrate, retell, and chronicle the past, as they were in the Middle Ages. Nor is there a simplistic desire to promote an ideology for the benefit of the contemporary world. The modern historian is driven by the desire to comprehend, to understand, the past. Herein lies its endless fascination, and the key to history.

The types of history and comparative history

Historians have an array of tools at their disposal

Historians are no longer limited to written sources and political history, but have access to a range of other disciplines and a wide variety of sources.

1. Literature, and foreign languages, geography, art, music, philosophy, sociology, anthropology, and archaeology – all have methods of which the historian can make use.

2. Comparisons across disciplines, and between historical epochs can illustrate and highlight similarities and differences.

3. Sources can be used from across the whole range of human activity: coins, architecture, tools, maps, household items, and the landscape itself.

History has begun to make use of every subject to give us a clearer picture of every aspect of the past. For example, literary criticism has shown the importance of considering the reader when writing a historical account. George Trevelyan was successful in this technique. Literary critics also remind us how to identify purpose, style, sarcasm and wit in the documents we evaluate. Historical literature itself is valuable, in that contemporary issues are revealed. Characters and events are often caricatures, not literally true. Like works of art they reflect the world they were created in. Charles Dickens and Thomas Hardy offer clues to life in Britain in the nineteenth century, whilst John Steinbeck in his novel *The Grapes of Wrath* tells us something about American views of the Depression. They are imprints for historians to interpret.

Approaching history in a practical way

The skills required

There are many skills that the historian needs:

1. The historian must be able to communicate, both in a written form and orally.

2. The historian must be numerate, especially when dealing with columns of figures, or items such as population statistics and currencies.

3. The historian must be able to use information technology, too, since many sources are now accessed this way.

4. The historian must also possess more traditional skills: a sense of curiosity about the past, an appreciation of human achievement and failure, a discerning attitude towards the sources, and a critical appreciation of the work of other historians.

Handling different types of sources with caution

Different sources require different approaches. Quantitative analysis for example demands a good grasp of mathematical models and graphs. Written sources pose their own kind of problems. Where sources have survived, the historian must be aware of what has already been lost and how this may affect the record.

Official government and diplomatic sources are valuable for indicating official public policy at a given point in time. Secret documents such as official memoranda may reveal a little more behind the scenes, but equally, both types might reflect only a view which was supposed to have been given.

Party manifestoes and pamphlets also give a flavour of a policy, but perhaps also reveal what the grievances and aspirations of an electorate may have been.

In the private sphere, letters can both mislead and reveal an honest conviction. The more intimate the letter, often the more personal the view held. Diaries also fit into this category, although there have been exceptions. For example the Nazi propaganda minister, Joseph Goebbels, kept a diary deliberately designed for public consumption at some later date.

Be cautious

Always be suspicious of memoirs. Authors may use selective memory, or try to present their role more sympathetically. Otto von Bismarck, the German Chancellor, claimed to have planned the unification of Germany from the early 1860s and to have orchestrated every move towards it. Yet events do not always seem to have turned out as Bismarck intended.

Photographs, too, can be unreliable. The Soviet Union frequently removed from official photographs individuals like Trotsky whom the regime had condemned. Never assume that your source is trustworthy. At the same time, even quite uninspiring documents may contain more than the first glimpse reveals. For more on how to analyse documents, read the next chapter.

Comparative skills are needed

It takes a great deal of skill to make comparisons effectively. The historian must take care not to stretch the similarity of different events, places and epochs too far. However, successful comparisons show how two or more systems may have worked, or the similarity of ideas. Always acknowledge the differences where they do exist. Then your reader will more readily accept the connections you make.

Analysis means asking questions

The next chapter examines the skill of analysis in more detail. Analysis is the single most important process and technique the historian uses. Essentially, an analytical approach means looking critically at the material, whether secondary or primary, and by asking questions. Working with others can stimulate more questioning. It is usual to end up with more answers than questions, but the process is challenging and keeps the subject fresh.

Tutorial: helping you learn

Progress questions

1. Why is important to strive for objectivity?

2. What is the value of subjectivity, and what are its limitations?

3. What skills do historians need?

Discussion points

1. How is it possible to avoid damaging, subjective judgements in history?

2. How far, if at all, can a more complete historical understanding be conveyed by drama, film or fiction than by 'standard' works of history?

Practical assignment

Compare the analysis of how history is carried out given in chapter one with the findings of this chapter. Compare your view of what history is with this analysis. Create a new summary on the value and method of history on no more than one page.

Study and revision tips

1. Avoid being too conclusive, and try to keep an open mind, when assessing causation, significance and objectivity.

2. Note that models of historical development, or 'laws', rarely match reality and are difficult to use when comparing different periods.

3. Always be cautious when handling and interpreting sources. Remain critical.

4. Be clear about your own philosophical approach to history and why you have adopted it.

6

Developing an Analytical Approach

One-minute summary – At advanced and higher levels of education, you will need to demonstrate the powers of analysis, not just remember detail. Narrative accounts of the past rarely achieve high grades. This reflects the importance of creating a commentary on the past whilst dissecting and examining the relative importance of different factors. The secret of success is to take an analytical approach to study, and present your findings in a sophisticated, analytical style. Look critically at the material you are dealing with, and ask questions. The questioning approach allows you to show your command of the material, your awareness of different interpretations, and to formulate a reasoned and rigorous conclusion. In this chapter you will learn about:

▶ using a balanced method

▶ reading critically

▶ taking notes to develop an analytical style

▶ taking a questioning approach

▶ writing analytically.

Using a balanced method

Study is the process by which you not only accumulate knowledge, but also understand it. If you simply read material, in time you will forget details. The time it takes to forget information is surprisingly fast. If you adopt the right technique, you can add to your store of knowledge and understanding without forgetting everything. The secret to this is the right balance of reading, reviewing and questioning.

Reading critically

Reading is essential
Reading is the single most important activity for the historian. It is vital to read widely. Reliance on only one text will be in danger of giving a distorted view of the topic. Failure to read the existing scholarship will mean that important debates will be missed and the reader will not be 'current'. Reading is essential to build up a picture of the topic and all its dimensions.

Reading with critical judgement
Reading is not a passive process. Your mind is digesting information, interpreting and evaluating. However, reading a historical text should be even more active. If we read, and simply accept what we read, we would soon realise that historians' interpretations conflict. If we took no further action, this would make life very confusing and frustrating. How then, do we make the right decision on who, or what to believe? The solution is to read with critical judgement. The same rules apply to historians (secondary sources) and original documents (primary sources).

Evaluate the author and style
First evaluate the author. Is it possible to establish the values and beliefs of the writer? If there is no dust-jacket information available, look at the preface, or the foreword (often written by someone else, but commenting on the author's relationship or views). Finally, assess the style of the language itself. By the end of the first chapter, it may be possible to discern certain revealing comments made by the author.

▶ *Example* – A. J. P. Taylor: the partiality of the author revealed. 'Nor shall I draw any moral which can be applied to foreign policy, or even to dissent, at the present day. In my opinion we learn nothing from history except the infinite variety of men's behaviour. We study it as we listen to music or read poetry, for pleasure, not for instruction.' A. J. P. Taylor, *The Troublemakers* (London, 1957) p. 23.

Alan Taylor liked to think of himself as the radical in the historical world. This extract is typical in that Taylor was content to give his opinion quite freely. Today, there is a convention not to use 'I', 'me', or 'my opinion' since it smacks of arrogance. To create the impression of impartiality, views and opinions are phrased impersonally:

'The most convincing argument is...'
'It could be argued that...'

The critical scholar has to be more alert to the historian's techniques of persuasion. Having established the authorship of the work, try to determine the author's motives. Is this a revisionist piece, overturning older, established ideas? Is it a call to arms? A response? A polemic?

What the text is saying, and why
The next stage is to establish what the text is saying. This is a combination of description, but also an opportunity to ask yourself: why has this section been included? What is the purpose of this piece of evidence? How accurate is this? How typical an example is it? What can you compare this with? What has been left out? These questions should be in your mind as you read. As you complete each chapter, revisit these questions. At the end of each section, jot down your conclusions in note form.

Targeting your reading is vital
You will be unable to read everything written on each subject, so it is vital to target your reading as much as possible. Do this by asking questions before you begin:

▶ *What is it that I'm trying to find out?* – Define the problem as clearly as possible, use a librarian to get you started, use the contents page for the whole context of an issue, and the index for specific references.

▶ *Is this the right source/book/journal article?* – Skim the contents, and one specific chapter to decide. 'Skimming' is a technique described below.

▶ *Can I break down the question I'm enquiring about, before I go any further?* – A vast subject like 'The Holocaust' is too broad. Try to establish some limitations to build out from. For example:

> The Holocaust
> > Origins?
> > > Ideas developed by leading Nazis from 1939 to 1943?
> > > How did the genocide begin in practice?
> > > Who else was involved?
> > > Who was, and what motivated, Heinrich Himmler?

The results of the first enquiry

As you complete these initial enquiries, jot down some of the key words
that you find. Leave space for your own thoughts too. All the time, keep
asking questions. Make a note of these for following up later. Your note
will begin to look like this:

Sample notes: raw data from reading [own questions in brackets]

Pre-Reading Questions
2. How did the genocide begin in practice?

June 1941, Russia invaded by Germany in Operation Barbarossa.
Troops were followed by special action squads and Security Police
(the SD).

There were orders to kill Commissars (Soviet political officers with
Russian army), Jews and partisans.

Police and SS killed large numbers by shooting.
    [how were soldiers persuaded to do this?]

Himmler was surprised by end of 1941 how few had died.

There was a conference at Wannsee to decide on new methods.
    [who ordered this?]

The result was the 'final solution': camps and gas chambers.
    [what were the other solutions? Why did they choose to use gas?
    Was the timing, when Germany was winning WWII,
    significant?]

The process of reading and how to improve it

Reading is a labour for the mind, and it is time-consuming. When the
eye travels over a line of text, it does not do so smoothly. It jumps from
one word group to the next and pauses for up to a fifth of a second to
process the information. The eye can also jump backwards and for-
wards over a sentence. Complex sentences are likely to increase the
'jumping back' of the eye:

WORD   WORD   WORD   WORD

By widening the span between pauses it is possible to read more quickly:

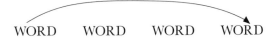

WORD   WORD   WORD   WORD

When we read, we tend to say the words 'aloud' in our minds. The solution is to skim over groups of words and avoid the temptation to return to areas you think you missed. Second, you should try to maintain a rhythm of eye movements. Some patterns for speed reading include:

1. The first and last line of a paragraph. In well-written work, the first sentence of a paragraph will usually announce what the paragraph contains. The last line will often conclude the idea of the paragraph, or link to the next paragraph. The technique is easy to use. It allows you to focus on areas on particular importance quickly.

2. The skimmed page. By moving the eye across the page evenly, in a diagonal, the brain will be able to absorb more than you think. This technique takes practice.

Reading critically

The next stage is to write down the key words. Key words are those that act like headings for important information. Consult this piece of text: a student, looking for information on the chief characteristics of the Holocaust, found the following paragraph:

> Racism was an essential component of Nazism. The racialist ideology reached its ultimate and terrible conclusion in the mass extermination of the Reich's enemies, the largest single group being the Jews. The term Holocaust, with all its religious and apocalyptic overtones, has been almost universally accepted as its description rather than the usual 'genocide'. The Holocaust sets Nazism aside as a different phenomenon than other preceding attacks on social groups because of its scale, and because of the 'scientific' justifications Nazis offered, and, most of all, because, as Volker Berghahn put it, 'it was the application of the processes of the production-line' to mass destruction. In 1945 it was termed a 'crime against humanity', and dealt a severe blow to the confidence of the West, and called into question its claim to civilisation.

The key words have been underlined. Stars, asterisks and lines in the margin can serve the same purpose. The key words serve to remind us of the entire text.

Recording the text is useful

The next stage is to record the key words, or data, in a summarised form. Traditionally, we rely on linear notes, distributed across a page in list form. Psychologist Tony Buzan (*Use Your Head*, 1974) established that the brain does not function in this linear way. By adapting the layout of notes to the way the brain operates, the notes become more effective. The following illustrates this point:

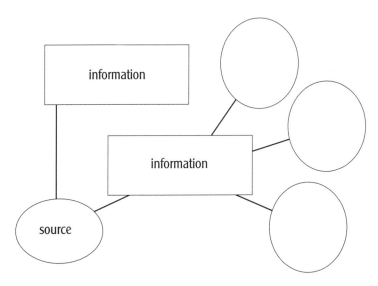

The brain stores information and retrieves it in a dendritic (tree-like) fashion, with branches emerging from each key word. Key words act as stimuli for more information. Information is also interconnected. Buzan believes our method of making notes on what we read should reflect this. Key words act like the nodes of information in our memory. They 'fire up' other areas of the brain, allowing us to retrieve far more. These notes are called mind maps.

Mnemonics act the same way as mind maps

The ancient Greeks understood this key word connectivity and introduced mnemonics to aid the memory. If the key words of the last example are used, their first letters form can be summarised as RHSSP. This could be turned into a 'word' to make it easier to remember: RHiSSP.

Suppose you were now to make a record of the topic 'The Holocaust'. A heading could be created in the middle of the page, and notes designed to flow from it.

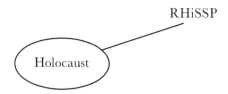

RHiSSP

Holocaust

This diagram can be extended as more information can be accumulated. The advantage of this system is that lots of information can be placed on to one page, allowing you to gain a clear overview of a mass of detail. Always leave space for your own thoughts, too. It would be a good idea to attempt the exercise at the end of this chapter called 'Key words and the mind map'.

Historical vocabulary should be tackled there and then
Whenever you come across a new, 'technical' term in the text, try to establish straight away what it means. These terms can be specific, general labels for ideas and movements, and metaphoric, for example, 'villein', 'feudalism', 'empirical', and 'anachronistic'. Historical and language dictionaries are useful here.

Conclusion: ask questions as you read
Passive reading is fine when you're reading for pleasure, but reading critically is vital in history. Don't worry if you end up with more questions than answers! These questions can form the basis of some stimulating discussions with others.

Reviewing
Unfortunately, it is impossible to retain detailed information for long periods of time, without some special techniques. If you were to take part in one session of learning, then in time very little of that information would be remembered. Look at the graph on the following page. This means that historians must make notes and periodically review them. To take one example, look at the deterioration of memory over time relating to the First World War on the following page.

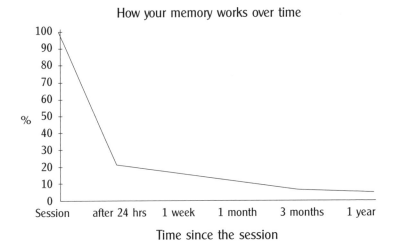

How your memory works over time

Example: The First World War: 1914

The session
* Germany developed and initiated the Schlieffen war plan to destroy French armies and envelop Paris
* German forces checked for 2 weeks at Liege
* Britain joined the war on 4 August 1914
* BEF [British Expeditionary Force] inflicted heavy casualties on German army at Mons and Le Cateau
* The German armies, although they advanced into France, lost cohesion
* German armies checked on the Marne
* Race to the sea [attempt to outflank the British] ends in stalemate and set back at Ypres.

What was recalled after one month
German war plan to destroy France
BEF [British Expeditionary Force] inflicted heavy casualties
German armies checked on the Marne

What was recalled after three months
Germans failed to destroy France in 1914
The British helped

What was recalled after one year
Germany failed to defeat France

How reviewing notes overcomes memory loss

Reviewing means skimming quickly over neat, well-prepared notes. If you have created summaries of each topic, it will be easy to 'fire-up' your brain and stimulate the memory. Skimming is rapid, thus avoiding the tedium of revisiting old material. It makes revision for exams more meaningful, too. Look at the following diagram:

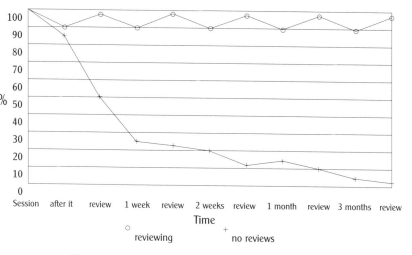

How reviewing memory overcomes memory loss

The first review
Note that the first review takes place the first evening after the session. At this stage it is a good idea to reform the key word notes you have made into a mind map with the key words highlighted in some way (see below for note-taking). Enter times for review on a year planner.

The second review (after one week)
Skim notes of keywords. Add details from later work on this topic. Try to create a summary or overview of the whole topic as soon as it is completed. Practise recalling your mind-map summary by memorising it, and trying to draw it out again without looking. What did you omit? Examine why you did not remember this detail.

The third review (after two weeks)
Skim your mind map summary, and once again add new material if necessary. Try to draw conclusions now on the topic.

The fourth review (after one month)
Follow the same procedure, but compare how memory loss is lessened compared with no review at all.

The fifth review
Skim notes again, and try re-drawing the mind map summary.

Conclusion: reviewing helps you to be analytical

The process of reviewing lets you retain material more easily. It also allows you to remember key arguments by other historians. This frees up more time for questioning, and for analysis. It helps you to deploy supporting material more relevantly too, helping you to develop an analytical style of writing.

Taking notes to develop an analytical style

Note-taking is a skill that takes time to master. The notes you take as a historian will cover lectures and seminar classes, written sources, and electronic sources.

Making notes from lectures and seminar classes

1. The only way to get the most from lectures is to do some preparatory work. Most courses provide reading lists, but if these are not available try to establish an overview of the whole topic and, if possible, the speaker's viewpoint.

2. Once you have completed some preparatory reading, jot down some questions that you have already noticed. If there is a chance at the end of the lecture, and the speaker hasn't covered it, you will be able to get them answered, or at least get the speaker's view. Note the date of the lecture, its location and the speaker's name.

3. In the lecture, don't try to write down everything that is said. Concentrate on the main themes that the speaker is putting across. Look for the key points of the argument.

4. If you have time, make a note of some of the examples the speaker uses, and the supporting detail, but continue to concentrate on the main ideas; you can get other details later.

5. Use lots of headings, colours, numbers and labels. Use underlining, lines in the margin, or asterisks to highlight important points.

6. Leave plenty of space for your own thoughts and assessment, which can be added at the time or later.

Making notes from written sources

(a) In the top left of your page, note author, title, publisher and date of publication. If the work is a later edition, note the edition you are using.

(b) Try to get an overview of the whole topic being addressed.

(c) Only include enough of the author's argument to enable you to recall it later. Don't try to write out too much.

(d) Look for the main ideas and key words. Look particularly for well-phrased points which could be used later as quotes. Always note the page number, frequently, in the margin.

(e) Keep your notes organised, legible and neat. This will enable you to absorb their contents more quickly, so you can spend more time thinking about what they mean.

(f) Create frequent summaries.

(g) Leave plenty of space for your own thoughts, ideas and questions.

Try to develop a shorthand of words and symbols for the most frequently used words. This will save you time. There are some examples at the end of this chapter.

Making notes from electronic sources

1. Make a note of the source you are using, the date and author (often at the bottom of the home page if it is a web site). Note the web address and the addresses of links that you visit. You can do this by bookmarking 'favourites' and downloading these later.

2. Download onto a disk only those pages which are strictly relevant. Create a folder for articles of the same type.

3. If using a CD rom, take notes just as you would for a written source.

Taking a questioning approach

History is not simply a question of assembling lists of events, or even of factors tied up with events. Narratives will not attract high grades.

▶ You will be expected to offer an evaluation.

To do this, throughout the process of reading and note-taking, it is important to keep questioning the material. Here is a list of questions to ask of sources.

Who wrote it? (what do we know of the background of the author?)

When was it written? (what else was happening then?)

Why was it written? (were there any special circumstances surrounding it?)

Who was it written for? (for whom was it intended?)

What does it say? (describe its contents, message and hidden meanings).

What doesn't it say? (what does it leave unsaid? Was this omission deliberate?)

What other sources do we have to compare it with? (can we corroborate its themes?)

Is it typical? (if exceptional, does it have validity?)

Is it reliable? (if unreliable, does it still tell us something about the past?)

What use is it to the historian? (is it significant? does it tell us something which is important?)

'Relative importance' is a good way to evaluate factors

If factors have to be presented, you will be expected to offer an assessment of their relative importance against each other. This is called relative importance. For example, if you were discussing the causes of the German Reformation, you would probably wish to include:

1. The early life and devotions of Martin Luther.
2. The widespread dissatisfaction in Germany with the sale of indulgences.
3. The corruption and worldliness of the church of Rome.
4. The secularising effect of the Renaissance on intellectuals.
5. The development of new theological ideas on salvation by faith rather than good works (the 'via moderna').

Simply listing these factors, without comment, will not be enough. List the factors in some kind of rank order. You could group them into their relative importance. For example, you might decide to put together factors 4 and 5 as background influences, 2 and 3 as reasons for the Reformation in the medium term, but 1 would be a 'trigger' cause. In this way, 4 and 5 could be seen as the 'origins' of the reformation, but 1, 2 and 3 could be seen as actual 'causes'. This is where the questioning approach can help. Having assembled the list in rank order, you may want to pose more questions: did this mean that the Reformation could have begun elsewhere? Why did it specifically begin when it did, and not before?

Historians must be able to conceptualise

Historians have to understand how ideas and models of the human condition work. It is important to understand what is meant by 'historical materialism', especially if you are examining a history written by a Marxist. It is vital to understand what is meant by 'revolution' when examining the origins of the French Revolution. This is because some concepts have affected the debate about these subjects. For example, the old interpretation of revolution was a recycling of an event, a return, in fact, to a previous state. Revolution in its more modern sense has come to be associated with the violent and bloody overthrow of power by large numbers of people. You must show that you understand and feel confident using concepts.

Look for the following examples, which tend to contain concepts:

causal relationships (how factors which caused an event interconnect)
consequences

comparisons
significance.

One way to test the significance of an event is to speculate on what would have happened had that factor been left out. Would it have made relatively little difference? If not, it probably is not the most important factor.

Writing analytically

Writing in an analytical style is far more effective than writing in a narrative style. Compare the following extracts:

Extract 1
The British empire expanded in the nineteenth century because of three factors. The first was military and naval power. Britain had a technological advantage over the states and tribal groups it encountered, and won a string of victories. Annexation of vast amounts of territory was achieved through military conquest. The second factor was trade. Britain's industrial revolution had created surplus manufactured goods and also a voracious appetite for raw materials. The acquisition of these raw materials tended to lead to the control of the lands where these could be obtained. To secure captive markets, there was another tendency to annex territory. The third factor was government leadership. Governments either openly espoused imperialism as a patriotic duty which would bring benefits to Britons and 'natives' alike, or felt that imperialism was a necessity in a commercial and military world that was increasingly competitive and threatening.

Extract 2
The reasons for the expansion of the British empire in the nineteenth century are not clear cut, and have provoked considerable debate amongst historians. Three factors are usually cited as being more important than the rest; military and naval power, the demands of Britain's commerce, and the role played by government. The first was certainly a catalyst factor in Britain's expansion, but cannot explain the reasons for it. Britain had a technological advantage over the states and tribal groups it encountered, and annexation of vast amounts of territory was achieved through military conquest. However, Britain had enjoyed a military and naval advantage over other states before, and yet there was relatively little expansion in the first half of the nineteenth century

compared with the previous one hundred years. In addition, some of Britain's annexations were not through conquest; Cape Colony became British following the Peace of Vienna in 1815. The second factor, trade, is also problematic. Britain's industrial revolution had created surplus manufactured goods and also a voracious appetite for raw materials. The acquisition of these raw materials could lead to the control of the lands where these could be obtained. To secure captive markets, there was also a tendency to annex territory. <u>However,</u> the lion's share of British trade went to America and Europe because they had the domestic market structure and demand for British goods. Colonial states simply could not afford the more expensive prestigious goods, and relied on massive British investment. The government of new colonies and their development was therefore expensive and to be avoided. It was thought far better to dominate their trade without the expense of occupation. Consequently this factor does not fully explain the reason for expansion and annexation, although it was an important precondition for the kind of annexation seen in the second half of the nineteenth century. The third factor was government leadership. Governments either openly espoused imperialism as a patriotic duty which would bring benefits to Britons and 'natives' alike, or felt that imperialism was a necessity in a commercial and military world that was increasingly threatening. This dichotomy compelled governments to intervene in areas previously thought to be worthless. For example …

Comment

Notice how the two accounts differ. The second is clearly more analytical, while the first simply lists factors. This analytical style is achieved by evaluating the factors (weighing up their relative importance) and conveying different opinions. For example, look at the use of the word 'however' (underlined). This is used to switch from one argument to the next. This can also be achieved with the following phrases:

On the other hand,
Conversely,
Nevertheless,
In fact,
Yet,
Whilst it could be argued that … , it would be equally valid to argue that …

Far from accepting this view, Dr Smith argued that ...
Notwithstanding,
Not only ... , but also
In contrast,
Despite
Although,
If, however, ...
Unlike ...

Conclusion

This chapter has discussed how to make your work more analytical. The key skill is to be able to question your sources as you read, whether those sources are primary or secondary. Note-taking is another opportunity for you to question, challenge, and constructively criticise. Reviewing not only allows you the chance to remember detail that would otherwise be lost, but it also gives you more time for reading, questioning and deciding on the meaning of the topic. As you read and note other historians' ideas, your own ideas will develop. These are important; they need to be recorded and used.

Tutorial: helping you learn

Progress questions

1. By what means does the historian 'target' his/her reading?

2. What methods can be used to aid the memory?

3. Why must historians be able to conceptualise?

4. How do historians make their writing more analytical in style?

Discussion points

1. Why isn't history simply a presentation of a series of documents for readers to discern for themselves?

2. 'All history is the history of thought'. Do you agree?

Practical assignment

Key words and the mind map: underline or highlight the key words in the passage below, and construct a mind map based on the key words.

The historical debate on the Holocaust
The historical debate over this aspect of Nazism is one of the most fierce. Memoirs continue to surface from survivors, or victims, and they mingle with those historians who have tried to explain the inexplicable – why did a modern, advanced and formerly democratic society turn to the barbarity of genocide? Who were the executioners? Lucy Dawidowicz wrote that the extermination of the Jews was both systematic and inevitable. These two simple words carry a whole range of questions which require consideration. At what point did the genocide become inevitable? What preconditions existed to enable this to happen? How was dissent silenced? How was it systematically organised? Does systemisation imply preplanning and the involvement of millions of people? Or only a handful of dedicated Nazis extremists?

Ian Kershaw addressed the problem from the point of view of the recent debate into how the Nazi regime functioned. There are historians who believe that the regime's leaders intended all that happened, and preplanned its agenda and simply put this into practice over the 12 years that it was in power. This is the Intentionalist view (supported by Dawidowicz, G. Fleming). The Structuralists (Hans Mommsen, M. Broszat) believe, by contrast, that it was the system that the Nazis constructed that created a dynamic of its own that no one person or group could halt, but was a by-product of half-baked ideas and vague instructions, or even no instructions at all. Kershaw, in a recent lecture, explained how he has recently explored the Soviet archives and discovered the reason why no order existed from Hitler ordering the mass extermination of Jews. This is tied in to the failure of the Euthenasia programme, and centres on a document dated 18 Dec 1941 from Himmler to Hitler, stating that the Jews are to be executed as partisans. Kershaw therefore modifies the intentionalist-structuralist debate, but really one should see him as part of the group that now feels that the Nazi regime was polycratic, and lurched between programmes, as rival groups fought for Hitler's approval. The 'polycrats' include Christopher Browning, Mary Fulbrook and Phillippe Burrin. Daniel Goldhagen (*Hitler's Willing Executioners*, 1996) joined this debate and claimed that all the Germans willingly joined in the orgy of violence against the Jews. He provided some useful new material on the ancillary staff of the Holocaust, particularly on the 'Death Marches' at the end of the war, but his thesis was weak in the following crucial respects: he refused to acknowledge the contrary evidence of German opposition to the regime, or the central role of Hitler, ideology, and the terrorising effect of the regime on ordinary citizens.

Study and revision tips

1. Review your notes and practise recall exercises at frequent intervals.

2. Keep your notes up to date and neat for ease of revision and review later.

3. Create a year planner and insert all key dates and reviews on it.

4. Have set times of the week for quiet study and for reading.

5. Try to spend some time each week just thinking through the issues by asking questions.

7

Examinations, Revision, Essays, and Dissertations

One-minute summary – Historians need to be highly organised if they are not to be overwhelmed with a mass of material. Creating an effective framework of study frees time from the mundane and less valuable tasks, so you can concentrate on the 'thinking' aspects of the discipline. There are many techniques in this chapter to help you become a more effective scholar. Amongst them are detailed and practical guides to planning and preparing essays and dissertations. The chapter, like the process, is developmental. These skills require practice, and the study skills should become a habit from the beginning. If you adopt these techniques, you will succeed. In this chapter you will learn about:

▶ developing an effective framework of study

▶ how to achieve higher grades in essays

▶ revision techniques to improve performance

▶ how to complete dissertations.

Developing an effective framework of study

There are two key problems associated with study for historians: access to materials and time available. The solution is to have an effective and well-organised programme. This can summarised as frameworks, organisation, concentration, and understanding.

Deciding your frameworks
Decide the best time of day for study. This varies with each individual. Some students find the best time for study is the mornings, others prefer to work in the evenings. Ensure the environmental conditions are right. If your study area is too hot, you'll feel drowsy; too cold and you'll be unable to concentrate. Make sure your workspace is well lit,

that your chair is comfortable, and that you have the materials you need to hand. Frameworks also include time. There may be deadlines to face. Mark them clearly on a year planner. Prioritise your time to allow a sufficient period for difficult work, or for assessed work. Decide your list of objectives for each time period.

Being organised

Keep clear notes, use a filing system that you understand, keep notes up to date and be aware of new developments in your topics (reading journals and book reviews are useful here). Keep a bibliography on each topic so that you can return to the work later. Make sure that you have a copy of the course details if you are following a set programme of study. Know the regulations of the institution you are working with. For example, there may be established ways of presenting your work.

Concentrating

Maintaining your motivation is vital. This can be achieved by balancing study commitments with exercise and rest.

Understanding

Consolidate your notes and carry out frequent reviews. Look up complex terms as soon as you meet them. Give yourself thinking time. For example, after studying a difficult section, take a quiet walk and try to think through the questions that it raises. Have a jotter pad by your bedside in case you a have a sudden inspiration during the night.

Recognising common pitfalls

It is tempting to procrastinate, or to carry out functional study tasks, in order to put off doing the difficult or meaningful work. On the other hand, fatigue or overwork can reduce your performance. Compiling notes, but never processing or reviewing them, are common errors, too. Scattered or disorganised notes will waste precious time. Reorganising them is a mundane duty that will kill off motivation. Avoid these pitfalls by following the guidance above.

How to achieve higher grades in essays

Too often, examination candidates try to impress an examiner by writing down everything they know about a topic. They fail to select what is relevant, or organise it in such a way as to answer the specific question that has been set. This goes for any essay, in fact. However, to achieve higher grades, do be aware of the following stages of writing:

1. Question analysis (determining what the question is asking, and thus what material is relevant).

2. Planning the relevant response with the right material.

3. Writing effectively with structure.

4. Concluding and checking.

Question analysis

Put simply, question analysis helps you to focus on the sort of answer required. It tells you what should be included, and what can be left out. It will also help you to design a line of argument.

► The objective of writing an essay is to examine your understanding and knowledge. It examines your ability to draw conclusions from evidence, your ability to evaluate opinions, your ability to select and organise relevant knowledge in order to answer a very specific question.

It is not acceptable to simply narrate factual information. Questions are framed deliberately as historical problems, rather than 'describe the events of ...'. At higher levels, questions usually ask you to evaluate, rather than explain.

Examples of evaluation questions

To what extent ...
What was the importance of ...
Assess the influence of ...
In what ways did ...
How successfully...
How far do you accept the view that ...
Compare the contribution of ...
What significance can be attached to ...
Consider the validity of ....
With what justification ... What was the importance of ...
Evaluate the ...
How true is ...

Describe and assess ...
Discuss the verdict that ...
Examine the claim that ...
Comment on the ...

The first stage is to underline the instruction part of the question, and
any key words which suggest the main area of study and the important
factors being presented. For example:

'In what ways, and to what extent, does the Marxist interpretation of
history remain of value?

This needs to be tackled as follows:

'In what ways, and to what extent, [the instructions] does the Marxist
interpretation of history [key phrase suggesting the main area for dis-
cussion] remain of value? [The question appears to suggest that there
is doubt about the value of Marxist history, offering the chance for
disagreement and support. The two sides of this argument will give
you a chance to develop an analytical approach to your answer.]

Paraphrase the question
The second stage is to paraphrase the question in your own words. Is
there a way of saying the same question in a different way? Make sure
you keep the main idea the same, though. Now ask yourself what is the
opposite viewpoint. Is it possible to present this? From your reading so
far, do you know of any controversies on this issue? The example may
now resemble this:

'It could be argued that the Marxist view of history is now invalid. It
was rigidly economically determinist and history rarely has one causation. It was a version of history promoted by the totalitarian Soviet
system. However, Marx's historical method did lead to the flourishing
of other historical ideas, especially the connection between economic
and social history. The question asks for an assessment to be made of
the Marxist method, and the legacy of Marxist history. This latter
point is the most important because it is asking for its effect on the
writing of history.'

This may appear long-winded, but you will now have a full idea of what
is to be included. Note that Marx also discussed the causes of revolution

and class struggle, the Asian economic system, the role of politics, and many other things but these may not be valid here. The question is specific; what Marxist history is and whether it still has value as a historical tool.

Asking questions to develop the analysis
As always, look for ways of asking further questions. If the Marxist interpretation is no longer valid, why not? What has replaced it? If Marxist history had not existed, would there have still been a development of economic and social history? What does Marxist history have to offer? Be realistic in your questions. Remember, key terms and concepts will need to be defined.

Transfer your analysis to a plan of argument
Now that you have established what the question is asking, think about what arguments can be developed from it. Decide on your own 'main argument'. Try to decide by saying aloud in one sentence what the answer to the question is. Then write it down. For example:

> 'Aspects of Marxist analysis have value to economic and social history, but it is still a poor model, and its determinism is off-putting to many historians.'

Try to contain your thoughts to this main argument. All the material you think you might use should support the main argument. Jot down a list of 6 factors you would include to prove that the argument is true or reasonable. If you have more than 6 main points, you can include them, but try to limit your essay plan at this stage so that you stay in control.

Consider balancing your argument
If you were to present only one argument, there is a danger that the essay will appear rigid and one-sided. Think about the opposite viewpoint. What material will you use to support this? You may decide to reject some ideas straight away, and to include ideas you disagree with in order to strengthen, and make more convincing, your main argument.

Planning your essay
Your 6 most important factors in support of your argument, and the opposing viewpoints, will now form the major paragraph headings of your essay. Each paragraph will deal with the issue you have raised.

Supporting and opposing material can be presented within each paragraph to achieve an analytical style.

Map out the six major points on a diagram

This will help you see the structure of the essay. You may alter the headings, discard some and add others, but you will now have a starting point. If you do discard a heading, ask yourself whether it still answers the question or not. Your initial diagram may look like this:

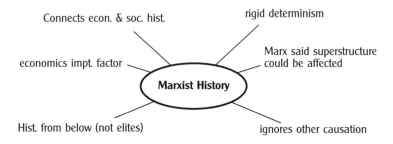

Preparation: make notes, select relevant material

If you do not have notes on the topic, you will now have a framework on which to base your reading and note-taking. Start by noting what you know about the topic already and your initial questions. Once you have accumulated notes on the topic, you will need to begin the process of selection.

Selection is the most difficult but also the most important part of essay-writing. If you were to organise your notes and simply write them up, your essay would be vast. You would lose important arguments in a morass of data. Selection shows consideration towards your reader. It is also fulfils the criteria on which you are examined: '... to select and organise relevant knowledge ...' So how do you select? The answer is to be ruthless at first. Ask yourself whether the information is an argument, or supporting information. Determine whether it directly supports or refutes the main argument.

Once you have these points, put them into a sequence. Make a note of the sequence and then try rearranging them another way. Numbering and colour-coding is helpful here. You could use blue for favourable ideas, red for opposing arguments, green for supporting data and quotes.

The more work you do now, the more time you will save when it comes to writing it up. It is important to know why you are including each point. Don't include points which you don't fully understand – go back and find out from your reading and your notes.

Make your points clearly

Historians must make clear the reasons for including their points. If data is included and the reader is left to decide what its relevance is, it is called 'implicit reference'. However, the reader is usually left wondering why that material has been included. The historian must therefore give the reason for putting the material there. This is called 'explicit reference'. Here is an example of implicit reference:

> 'The first Dreadnought was launched in 1906, and in 1907 the Germans launched their own ship of a similar design called the Nassau. By 1914, Britain had 19 Dreadnoughts, whilst Germany had 13.'

Notice how there seems to be little point to the inclusion of the material. Compare this with the following example of explicit reference.

> 'The Royal Navy's *concern* that Germany was challenging Britain's naval supremacy *was based on* the fact that Germany had launched her own version of the revolutionary new Dreadnought class just one year after the British had done. Germany and Britain were locked into a naval race and by 1914 Britain was marginally ahead with 19 at sea, whilst Germany had 13.'

The words in italics show where the explicit reference has been made.

Every argument and point must be supported by evidence

Rather as in a court of law, historian must be able to justify their arguments. This is done by using supporting evidence. On the plan that you have made, list the headings of the supporting evidence that will appear. Once again, it is important to select evidence. When dealing with controversies, always try to include the historians (names and works) to acknowledge the effort put into this topic already. You can quote brief passages where you feel that the problem has been summed up particularly well. It is more usual to quote historians that you disagree with, in order to acknowledge their contribution, but to courteously point out their omissions, or to present a new angle. Remember, to do this your evidence must be clear cut, and you will need to suggest a solution. Be cautious in your criticism: many of those you disagree with will have spent many years researching the same material.

An example of a statement and supporting evidence
Here is an example of an unsupported statement:

'By the 1470s, the effects of overall economy – better management, better accounting and cuts in unnecessary expenditure – were such that the king was able to start paying off old debts.'

This version includes the supporting evidence:

'By 1471 and 1476, debts owed to Gerard Canizani, the agent of the Medici, were reduced from £14,390 to £3,000. In 1478 the king was able to assign revenues to pay off the whole of his debt of over £12,000 to the City of London. In 1466 he had owed nearly £33,000 to Calais ...[this was reduced] to a mere £2,000. Edward died solvent, which none of his Lancastrian predessors had done.'
M. H. Keen, *England in the Later Middle Ages* (London, 1973) p. 498.

Writing the introduction
The introduction is perhaps the most crucial part of any piece of written work. Historians sometimes write the introduction after they have written the rest of the essay, or, at least, redraft it several times. The introduction does not introduce the background to the period. Its purpose is to introduce the main argument. The easiest way of starting an essay is to write down your answer to the essay question in one sentence, the same one that you said out loud to yourself and wrote down during the planning. The introduction is a statement of intent; it tells the reader where the essay is going. That is not to say that you need to laboriously give all your headings in a list. However, throughout the essay you must stick to the main argument in your introduction, and of course stick to the question set.

The parts of an introduction and how they work
The parts of the introduction and their purpose are as follows:

▶ *An assessment of the question* – This shows that the writer has understood the theme of the question and knows what the topic is about, including the slant that the question may be putting on this topic.

▶ *Line of main argument and ideas* – This outlines how the writer will proceed and how the main argument works. It will also be a chance to show opposing views. If there has been a historiographical debate, there is a chance to show that the writer understands this problem and its context.

▶ *Transition to the essay* – This will map out the direction of the essay, and if necessary, explain the definitions that have appeared in order to show how they will shape the essay at this point.

Writing the introduction

As a rule of thumb it is useful to write two sentences under each of the categories above. The assessment of the question, therefore, is made up of two sentences. You can choose to attack the slant of the question from the outset, but if you do take care not to appear too dogmatic, or to attack the person who has posed the question. Be brief. Be concise.

Style is important

Style varies with each person, but there are some useful ground rules for style. Remember that good style helps the reader, thus making your views more accessible. The rules are as follows:

▶ *Accuracy* – Inaccurate history is distracting and irritating. Checking details before putting pen to paper is essential. Having others check your work is useful, but it is your responsibility to ensure that your work is accurate.

▶ *Brevity* – When you lack confidence, it is easy to pad out your work with irrelevant details in the hope of making the essay look more authoritative. This rarely works and will only waste your time. Look back over the section on planning the essay. When you have written a first draft, check each sentence and ruthlessly remove all those that add nothing to the main arguments.

▶ *Clarity* – This is best summed up in George Orwell's five rules for clarity:
1. Never use a long word where a short one will do.
2. Do not try to impress with words which sound pompous and inappropriate. Shorter words take less time to read and are clear.
3. If it is possible to cut out a word, cut it out.

4. Get to the point.

5. Never use a foreign phrase, a technical word or a jargon word if you can think of an everyday English equivalent. (NB: the only exception is where you are using concepts and terms specific to the question. For example, if you were discussing the Nazi seizure of power, words such as Machtergreifung and Gleichschaltung would be acceptable.)

▶ *Never use the passive voice when you can use the active voice* – It is clearer to avoid 'had been' in favour of 'did'. For example, 'Some historians have been considering the question as to how far the British empire had been declining before 1914'. Change this to 'Historians have considered whether the British Empire was in decline before 1914.'

▶ Break any of these rules rather than produce barbarous writing.

Reiterating, signposting and paragraphing are important

During your essay, refer back periodically to the question. Reiterate the main argument, but do not repeat the same words. Show how each example you are using reinforces your main idea. Don't feel this has to be done after every paragraph, but at convenient points, and major junctions in the essay. These will act as signposts for your reader.

The same effect can also be achieved with good paragraphing. The first line of each paragraph should show what the paragraph contains. The middle of the paragraph will be an opportunity to make the argument clear and to present supporting evidence. It will also be the chance to deal with opposing views. The final line of the paragraph should either (1) link to the next paragraph or (2) close that idea that was introduced in the first line.

Check some of your written work now. Do your first lines introduce the rest of the material in that paragraph? Avoid one-sentence paragraphs. This may work in novels where a dramatic effect is required, but it is a weakness in history writing. Paragraphs are the means by which you provide supporting evidence for your argument. They should also be broadly chronological, even when the essay is clearly thematic in approach.

Be in command of your language: punctuation and spelling

Control of your language is essential to write well in history. Punctuation is like the pauses you take when you talk, so a good way of checking whether the punctuation is right is to read it aloud. If you stumble when you read it, it is probably an error of punctuation.

Good history can be ruined by poor punctuation, because the impact of an argument can be completely lost. The reader becomes confused or gets lost. The result is that they fail to be convinced by the argument. As a rule of thumb, keep sentences short, but add one or two longer ones for variety. Re-read this paragraph and examine the length of each sentence. You will notice the effect that punctuation has on what you read.

Be aware of your spelling, too. Spell-check has assisted the historian a great deal, but you will still need to check your essay through at the end. It is very easy to let spell-check take over and turn the eminent British prime minister, William Gladstone, into William Gallstone! Poor spelling, especially of historical names and places, is a distraction and is inaccurate. Inaccuracy in spelling will make your reader wonder what else is inaccurate, including both your argument and your evidence. Finally, never use abbreviations in your essay. Write 'for example', not 'e.g.'. Do not use '&', but 'and'. It is very easy to make a mistake and transfer abbreviations from your notes; the solution is to check over your work at the end.

Concluding your essay

Your conclusion is as vital to the success of your essay as your introduction. It has two functions:

1. It allows you to restate the main argument as an explanation for the answer you have given.

2. It allows you to explain how and why the answer you have given differs from, or changes, the slant given in the question itself. If there was no slant, you will be able to explain how and why your view differs from other arguments.

Refer to the question in your conclusion and refer to your intentions as laid out in the introduction. Avoid simply listing what has already been said, and definitely avoid phrases like 'thus it can be seen that ...'. As a general guide, about 6-7 sentences would be fine. At all costs avoid contradiction. If appropriate, finish with a hypothesis, or suggest how the topic made a contribution to a later period. However, unless you are dealing with a contemporary history topic, avoid leaping to the conclusion that your topic shaped the present day. Avoid this:

'Therefore Louis did a good job, although in many things he failed.' (contradiction)

Instead consider something like this:

'The significance of Louis's reign is that we observe not a medieval king but a ruler of the threshold of the modern world.'

Another method would be to finish with an appropriate quotation, either from a contemporary or a historian.

Common errors to be avoided

1. One common error is not sticking to the aim of the essay, and becoming over-enthusiastic about how much to include.

2. Another is forgetting to support each argument with evidence. This usually results in generalisations of little value, instead of developing specific points.

3. It is easy to overlook acknowledgement of other historians, or even to attribute to them views which they do not hold. This is often reveals that too little reading has been done.

4. Avoid contradictions within your own arguments – check your essay carefully.

5. Spelling errors can be detected by careful checking, too.

6. It is important to make the essay the right length. An issue that often concerns students is how much to write. The simple way is to ask whoever is setting the work how many words are required. In an hour-long examination, for example, it would be reasonable to write about a thousand words.

Plagiarism is a crime

The worst crime in historical writing is plagiarism. This is where someone has copied whole lines, passages, or even ideas without ac-knowledging the source. It is the equivalent of academic fraud, and very serious indeed. Never do this. Equally, you should resist the tempta-tion to steal lines and simply change one or two words to conceal the source. The penalties are severe.

Examination coaching is about rehearsal

Prepare for the examination well in advance. Start about six months before by deciding on what areas of the examination you will concentrate on, and what topics will be your back-up ones in case the first choices fall through. Revision techniques are covered later in this chapter.

In the examination, calculate how much time you have to spend on each question. Stick to this rigidly or you will run out of time for the final question which may carry the same marks as the first ones.

Spend about five minutes planning each question carefully. Jot down the arguments, and use mnemonics to remember the supporting factors. Remember to limit the number of examples/points to what can be realistically tackled within the time available. Do not worry about not including everything; the examiner will be expecting a selection.

Make all your decisions about the examination essay before you start writing your introduction. Write the essay, periodically checking the time and the plan. Once you have finished, read the whole essay through from the start. Concentrate on three things: clarity of argument, spelling, and punctuation.

Document questions have a distinctive style

A common style of examination question is the document question. Here, one or more extracts from original sources are presented along with a series of questions. Often low scoring questions come first, so don't neglect the later questions, or spend too much time on the first ones. The key to scoring good marks is to avoid simple descriptions of what the document contains. If you know the context, you will be expected to say something about it.

When referring to the extracts, don't waste time by writing out large sections of it. Refer to line numbers instead, or, if these aren't available, the opening clause of a sentence you are referring to. Make references to the text wherever you can. You may be asked to contrast (find differences in) and compare (find similarities) in extracts. Do not stray beyond these instructions: refer to as many factors as possible and which are appropriate within them.

If you are invited to discuss the context of the document, do not waste time referring to other texts, but explain the background to the document, that is to say, 'where does it fit in a wider history' and 'why is it significant?'. If you are asked about the usefulness of a particular extract, consider what we would not know, had the document not existed. State its significance to the topic as a whole.

Revision techniques to improve performance

Preparation is the key

History examinations involve remembering a lot of material. It is easy to forget the vital importance of focusing on arguments. Learning factual detail tends to channel you into narrative responses. Examinations are less a test of your knowledge, than of your understanding. Learning answers for a particular essay, which you hope will turn up, is also counter-productive: your answer will probably end up mechanical and simplistic. The secret is to stay flexible.

Try to acquire some recent examination papers. Examine how each question is phrased. Experiment with the different responses you could give to each. When you have completed a revision topic, practise writing an essay under timed conditions. Be critical of your performance. How successful was your time planning, your main argument, and the quality of your evidence? Keep up to date, too. The most recent views will show that you are 'current'.

Regroup your notes to avoid the narrative trap

Simply reading through your notes is a passive exercise. It might be one way of acquiring knowledge, but it will not develop your skills of analysis. J Black and Donald Macraild (*Studying History*, 1997) suggest you try regrouping your notes under the following headings:

1. Introduction and Overview (what are the general themes and issues?)
2. Historiography (how has the writing on this topic developed?)
3. Theories (are there social/political/economic theories associated with the topic? How useful or valid are they?)
4. Controversies (where do historians differ?)
5. Sources and methods (what have the different approaches been?)
6. Events and incidents (how do key events help us to understand the topic?)
7. Conclusions (importance, perspectives, overviews of the topic)

Recall exercises are valuable

Once you have thought about the topic this way, and you have learned some of the factual material, you will need to reduce it into a manageable form. Mnemonics and buzzwords, which stimulate the memory, will help you to remember lists. Create mind maps with the major headings listed along branches, and embellish them with further details as sub-branches. You may be able to reduce whole topics onto a sheet of paper. Once you have completed a revision session (no longer than 45 minutes, to aid concentration), take a break: when you return try to write out the mind map again. Look for ways of linking information. Try filling in two columns on a side of paper showing comparative and contrasting relationships. Once again, once completed, try to draw it out again on a fresh sheet of paper. Check over what has been missed out. Commit yourself to remembering these details.

Quotations have to be learned

Quotations have to be learned rather differently, like the lines of a play. This need not be passive either. A handful of flexible but memorable ones can be learned by re-reading and memorising. Word association and picture images can also help you to remember: simply associate the full quotation with a picture or a word in your mind. Pinning individual quotes on small cards on everyday objects can also help. A list of ten points, or quotes, on a pad of paper by the bedside can be read once through every night and every morning. In time, a new list will be possible as the points are remembered.

Practise questions with others

A valuable way of learning and remembering is to learn with someone else, as long as you have both prepared the first stage of the material. Practise essay plans and read them aloud. What has been missed out? Can the main argument be justified?

How to complete dissertations

Preparation and planning is the first step

The dissertation is the longest piece of work that university students have to write. For undergraduates, the length will be around 10,000 words, rising to 40,000 for MA graduates and 80,000 for PhDs. Dissertation titles are the choice of the student. Wherever possible the research should be original, that is, it should cover new material. However, there is the chance to apply new theoretical ideas to, or to re-examine, topics that have the subject of earlier research. The boundaries of these approaches are not mutually exclusive, and combinations have been very successful. Your choice of topic will be very important. Try not to tackle too broad a subject. Choose your area of study on the basis of the following:

1. What advice can you get from a tutor on what to study?

2. What sources are available, and where are they held? Are you prepared to travel to see them?

3. Will language be a barrier? Are translations available?

4. Can you focus your interest into a smaller area of research?

5. How much work has been done on this topic already?

6. If you decide to concentrate on a small case example, will you be able to relate this to a wider context?

Creating an outline

Having answered these questions, you are in a position to create an outline, including:

(a) A skeleton plan of the chapters and their contents.

(b) A single side describing the main argument and how this subject will be interpreted. This will help to clarify what you are hoping to study. You will be asked to submit this quite early on, so try to get a grasp of the whole topic area in outline quite quickly.

(c) A plan of work, including completion dates, fees and costs (such as travel). The plan will change as ideas develop and reading proceeds, but the outline will keep all its aspects in perspective. A diary of development will be a good place to log what you have done and new developments in the study. New ideas can be recorded for follow up later too. You will probably have twelve months to complete the dissertation (if you are a full time student), but each phase will take some time, so divide the time carefully. Aim to get the bulk of the primary research done as soon as possible, but after the initial secondary reading.

The process of research is development

Do not think that reading, archival research and writing up are distinct phases which only begin once the other has stopped. In fact, they overlap considerably. A useful tactic is to start with some general secondary reading, taking notes throughout. After a short time, you should draft up what you have read. After each book, write a paragraph summing up its main thesis. These records should then be carefully stored and retrieved to compare with new notes and other reading. The same process should take place with archival research. Having completed an analysis of each document, or volume of materials, write up the general themes and crucial details. Writing will helps crystallise your ideas, and make discussions with your supervisor more meaningful.

By the six month point, you will need to have completed the bulk of your reading and archival work. Once you reach this point, try drafting more detailed chapter outlines (a side of A4 at least). Concentrate on argument, but include the most crucial sources you will include in outline.

By the nine-month point, you should have written a draft of the first two chapters which you may be able to get some advice on. Get plenty of advice from your supervisor, and meet at regular intervals. Be honest with the supervisor, and solve problems as they appear; don't try to avoid them. Keep to a routine of a half day for the dissertation each week to assist you in developing a work habit. It's a lonely business, it's easy to feel isolated, but keep going: you can do it, and you will make it!

Developing a theme

The chapters of a dissertation are like essays in themselves, but linked by a common theme as outlined in your introduction. The introduction will tackle the recent historiography that is relevant to the topic, explain why the topic is important, and how your work will contribute to our understanding of it. Once again, put emphasis on your main argument and its context. Check that the meaning of what you are saying is clear.

Briefly explaining your methodology can be helpful, and in some institutions it is expected. If not, you can include an appendix covering this, so that you concentrate on the main argument. Acknowledge the theoretical approaches to the topic.

Be honest about what you have not included, so that you are judged on what you have said, rather than what you have omitted by accident. Throughout, try to reiterate your main idea. Link your chapters together by reference to your main argument. It is a good idea to point to what comes in the second chapter at the end of chapter one. In the same way, chapter two should begin by picking up the thread from the first chapter.

Writing a conclusion

Dissertations are often concluded rather badly. Hard-pressed scholars seem to heave a sigh of relief as they approach the finishing line. It is worth pausing before writing your conclusion. Plan it carefully after reading through the whole dissertation from start to finish. Consider drawing together what you have written, and relate it to the historiography that you have introduced. How does the topic you have discussed fit into a wider context? What value are your conclusions to other aspects of the topic?

How to present your work: conventions on format

History has certain conventions which aid clarity. The format for dissertations should be as follows:

Title page
(Abstract, if required)
Contents
List of illustrations (plates, figures, maps)
(Foreword, if a book)
Author's preface
Acknowledgements
Glossary and abbreviations (can be before the bibliography at the end)
Introduction
Chapters
Appendix
Notes and references
Bibliography (subdivided into primary and secondary materials, in alphabetical order)
(Index, if a book)

Conventions on quotations, margins, and footnotes/endnotes

Quotations of more than five lines should be indented and set off from the main text. They should be enclosed in single speech marks. Quotes within quotations should have double speech marks. Shorter quotations can remain in the text within speech marks. All quotations should be given a footnote reference and the source cited. Be accurate. If you need to shorten the quote to make it clearer, then use three dots to indicate what has been left out (like ... this).

A margin of one inch should be left on the left side of the page. Typed worked should be 1.5 or double-spaced. Handwritten work should always be double-spaced.

Footnotes or endnotes are used to acknowledge the source from which they are taken. Authors, books, articles, and ideas should all be cited. Authority for controversial statements, and any ideas that are not the writer's own, even if not directly quoted, should be footnoted. Information which is commonly known, or available from encyclopedias, need not be footnoted. Footnotes can also be used to amplify statements in the text which are important, but which, if included, would detract from the main argument. Footnote reference numbers should be placed at the end of the sentence or passage. Footnotes appear at the bottom of the page on which the reference occurs, unless it is an endnote, in which case it must be clearly labelled by chapter at the end of the work.

The form footnotes take
The first time a reference is cited it should include author, title (*italics* or underlined) followed by place and date of publication in brackets and the page number(s). All subsequent references can have an appropriate shorter form. If the second reference follows immediately, the writer can use the term 'ibid.' and add the new page number.

(1) W. G. Hoskins, Middle England (London, 1949) p. 16.
(2) Ibid., p. 17.

If there are intervening references, a second or subsequent reference would appear with the author, a short version of the title if necessary, and the term 'op. cit.,' with the page number at the end.

(1) W. G. Hoskins, *Middle England* (London, 1949) p. 16.
(2) R. W. Dunning, *Local History for Beginners* (Chichester, 1973) p. 10.
(3) Hoskins, op. cit., p. 17.

Figures generally should be written in words
Figures under one hundred, and larger figures that are round numbers should be written in words, for example, one thousand men. Sums of money are written in figures, for example, £1,000. Percentages are expressed in words, not with a % sign. Dates are written in full in the text, and centuries are expressed the same way. You can abbreviate dates in the footnotes, but be consistent. Year sequences are expressed as 1816-17 (years 0 to tens), 1866-7 (following years not tens), 1885-95 (gap is over ten years), 1898-1905 (new century).

Bibliographies must be precise

Books are cited alphabetically by author's surname, followed by the initials, the book title (underlined or in *italics*), and the place and date of publication in brackets. Where there are two authors, only the first cited is surname, then initials, the second is cited with initials and then surname. Journal articles or individual chapters are given in single speech marks followed by the reference in which the article appears. Articles are followed by the date of publication, a colon and the page numbers. British students should refer to the *MHRA Style Book* (London, 1991), and American students should consult the *MRA Handbook* (New York, 4th edn, 1995).

> Bloggs, Frederick, *History of the World*. 2 vols., (London, 1932)
> Blackguard, J. and Hugh Jekyll, *The Historians*. (USA: Harvard, 1999)
> Crosby, B., 'A wartime Christmas' in R. Hope, ed., *The War Years*. (USA: Lincoln, 1944)
> Potemkin, A., 'The Mutiny' in *Journal of Eastern European and Slavonic Studies*, 16 (1945): 123-46.

Conclusion

This chapter is a quick guide to good writing, but proficiency will only come with practice. Plan carefully. Remember that historical writing is not a factual or narrative list. Adopt an analytical style by questioning and presenting two or more sides of the debate. Concentrate on being concise. Use simple words, the active voice, and leave out unnecessary words to achieve clarity. Be accurate; check what you have written before submission. Get advice at frequent intervals. If you are preparing for examinations, start early. Get organised. Rearrange your notes to make analytical judgements. Do not be passive and try to absorb factual information, but be active instead. Practise recall exercises. Try to remember controversies and a handful of meaningful quotations to add a little style to your work.

Tutorial: helping you learn

Progress questions

1. What is the purpose of question analysis?
2. Why are six paragraphs recommended when planning an essay?

3. How do historians create 'explicit reference'?

4. How do you refer to the specific parts of a document question during an examination?

Discussion points

1. Are dissertations, in reality, limited to an empirical approach?

2. In how many different ways can an essay or dissertation be concluded?

Practical assignment

Create a mind-map summary diagram to make notes on this chapter, and to remember its contents. Use an A3 sized sheet if necessary.

Study tips

1. Prepare your notes carefully. They are the foundation of your written work.

2. Remember to select evidence and historical examples. Your work is not just a test of knowledge.

3. Apply the feedback you get from each essay.

4. Check to see that your main argument is stated in your introduction.

5. Make sure the reader knows why each you have included each piece of evidence.

6. Back up every statement with evidence.

7. Read widely to give your work more breadth, and to improve your historical knowledge.

8. Check your English, as well as the historical content, before you hand work in.

9. Stick to the structure of your plan and the question.

10. Use your conclusion to reiterate your main argument, and say how and why it satisfies the question.

8

Research and Retrieval

One-minute summary – Electronic sources are useful ways of saving time and making searches for material more comprehensive. So much material now exists that, unless you can access information efficiently, you will be overwhelmed by it all. Worse, perhaps, you will be unaware of new developments. Learn, and practise, how to use the 'search string' techniques. Be aware of what electronic sources have to offer. Historians can no longer afford to be computerphobes. A failure to be computer literate today is the equivalent of basic illiteracy in previous generations. In this chapter, some guidelines for visiting and using archives are included. In this chapter you will learn about:

▶ research and retrieval using books and journals

▶ accessing electronic sources

▶ trawling the world wide web

▶ using archives.

Research and retrieval using books and journals

Library books: Boolean searches explained

The fastest way of getting to the material you want is by electronic means, rather than walking along the library shelves in the vain hope of spotting something useful. Libraries use a 'Boolean' technique to help you reach your material. (Boole was an English mathematician.) The first stage is to type in the word which most approximates to your area of interest. This is known as a 'search string'.

▶ *Example* – If you were trying to find out about the development of the German navy prior to the first world war your search strings might be: navy, or battleships, or Germany.

However, these strings will give you a wide number of areas so it would be useful to narrow the search using AND, OR and NOT. AND indicates that you want both of these terms of reference in the search. OR tells the system to search for references which have either one or the other terms. NOT tells the system to leave out all references with a particular term. The notation * indicates that the word ending is not crucial and the search should look for all the word endings for that stem. This is called stemming. For example, 'nav*' could be naval, navy or navigation. The search string could now look like this:

nav* OR Wilhelmine AND Germany

You need not limit yourself to single words. You can bracket words together if you want information on a variety of areas. For example, you could ask for:

(International/global/European) OR (American)

If there are different spellings of a words, or foreign word equivalents, these can also be bracketed. The '/' sign acts the same way as the OR command. In some systems, a comma is used, so check the menu first. Similarly, AND can also be written as + or sometimes as &.

Refining your search and retrieving the book

When your first set of responses returns, you may need to refine your search still further, or rephrase terms if they don't appear to be successful. A little time spent here will save a lot of legwork, though. The responses, or 'hits', will offer you a minimum of information, but options are offered for you to find out more about the book (and therefore make sure it is the one that you are after).

Make a note of the class mark number, author and title. It is in this order that you will find the item on the shelf. Most stacks of shelves have the class mark numbers written clearly above them, for example: 941.81-942. Go to the stack within the range indicated. You can count along the shelves to home in on the class mark number on the book you are looking for. Author and title details will confirm it is the right one. At this point it is a good idea to take a quick look at the book's contents, layout and index. Books that are missing may be on loan (you can check this at the computer too) and you can reserve them. Alternatively, if your library does not hold a book, it is possible to use an inter-library loan system, but you may have to pay for it.

Journals
BIDS helps you find

BIDS stands for Bath Information and Data Services. It is an online search system for some 7,500 journals worldwide. To use BIDS you have to belong to a subscribing academic institution, and have been issued with a password and username. If you have not used the system before, there is a useful guide available from the subscribing institutions. Essentially, BIDS works the same as the standard Boolean search. Note that other useful symbols to put in search strings are # (meaning AND, OR, or any other word that could go between), ? (which can substitute for a letter, hence wom?n could be woman or women), and _ can be used to separate names from initials (for example, Hopkirk_P). BIDS also has a citation index, so if you know of the journal details already, you can use this index to go straight to it. You could then widen a search from there.

FirstSearch is a massive online database

FirstSearch is a service provided by OCLC (Online Computer Library Center Inc.) and has over 50 databases. Like BIDS, to use FirstSearch you need to be part of a subscribing institution, but there are no access passwords. Articlelst contains over two million records from 12,500 journal titles from 1990 or 1992. PapersFirst contains citations on papers given worldwide at conferences, workshops and symposia since October 1993. ProceedingsFirst gives citations on publications from worldwide conferences from 1993. SocsciInd is an index of 350 social sciences publications. Contentslst contains the complete table of contents of 12,500 journals. As with Articlelst, most of these begin in 1990.

Finding journals: BHI and Wilson HI

The British Humanities Index and the American Humanities Index are known respectively as BHI and Wilson HI. These can access all journals except those published in the previous ten days. American journals, once identified, can be purchased via the BIDS system.

Accessing electronic sources

Searching CD roms
Searching a CD rom is slightly different from the standard Boolean search. You cannot put the whole search string in, but have to work in

stages. First enter the term or terms separated by ORs. The computer will carry this out and give you a number of hits. You can refine the search by a second round of ORs. Only when you have narrowed the search as fully as possible with ORs, should you commence the search using AND. You can then further refine your search using dates of publication and so on. Some useful CD rom material includes an *Index of Theses*, *The Oxford Dictionary*, *Hansard* (parliamentary debates), *The Times* and *The Sunday Times*.

Search strings can be cribbed

Choosing the right words for a search string is important. You can select terms using your imagination or a dictionary (if more technical), but the first few rounds of hits will also suggest new ideas. For example, your first round of hits may tell you that there were 75. Only the first few will be displayed on the screen. You could scroll through them all, but to save time you could narrow your search. Look at some of the titles, are there any clues to new search strings you could use?

Refining your search still further

The process of adding more limitations to the search is called filtering. You have successfully narrowed your subject word search, but the historiography is so vast it is unmanageable. In this case you could limit the number of hits by selecting books after a certain date of publication. You can do the same with the type of publication, and its language. If you are short of time, you can download the hits onto a disk and browse them at leisure. This has the added benefit of allowing you to transfer the titles you do use straight onto a bibliography. If you can download them, you can sometimes email them to your own email address. With CD roms you will probably have to tag/mark hits before you download them.

OPAC: the British Library Service can help you

The British Library has placed catalogues of many of its holdings of books, journals, conferences and theses online. You can search these using foreign languages instead of English. If you were trying to locate original documents, the system will help you. For example, if you wanted to find out what sort of pamphlets were written during the period of the Great Reform Act of 1832, you could select publications after 1831 and type the search string 'reform'.

NISS: the university library gateway is a powerful tool

NISS is a service that operates as a gateway into the holdings of university libraries in the United Kingdom. This allows you to search through another libraries' shelves without actually being there. However, not every institution is online and some have different codewords for their online system, so check their menu and make a note of the differences. Unfortunately, you have to access one institution at a time and carry out the same search each time, so it can be time-consuming.

Trawling the world wide web

For searches on the internet use Boolean techniques

Essentially the system of searching on the internet using the Boolean method is the same. It is advisable to try one or two different search engines if possible, as results can vary. Many academic institutions are establishing their own intranets which filter information from the jumble of the web into manageable and organised spheres. The key to success can often rely on gateway sites. Some sites, with good links, are listed at the end of this book. Allow plenty of time for internet searches, and try to work quickly. Discard anything which appears of only marginal relevance, stick to the search in hand; it is easy to get sidetracked by related but unhelpful information.

Information on archives is available on the web

The world wide web is a useful way of finding out more about the archives that you may need to visit in the course of your research. Opening times, closures for holidays, access and costs can be researched, and, sometimes, even enquiries (as with the Public Record Office at Kew) can be answered.

Using archives

Locating the archive

Locating the archive that you need can be a difficult task. A helpful first step for British papers would be to contact the National Register of Archives. If you are carrying out local research, many of Britain's county towns house a local history collection. Each county has a historian, and often a team of archivists, to help you. Museums can also be fruitful, too. Two of the biggest collections of papers in Britain are the Public Record Office at Kew and the British Library near St Pancras

Station in central London. Scotland has its own collection in the National Library of Scotland in Edinburgh. The staff are always polite and helpful, and the systems of delivering documents to you are breathtakingly efficient. Another place to find the relevant collection would be the bibliographies of academic books and journals.

Getting access to the archive

The first step is to write for permission. Some archives accept an email application, but it is more usual to write. Be concise, but specific about your field of research. This will enable the archivist to direct you more quickly to the right place. They will also be able to save you time; it just might be that the part of the collection you are hoping to see is housed elsewhere. Find out the opening times. Many are shut during the Christmas and Easter periods for a few days. Identification is often required, and cards are frequently issued to researchers for security.

Using the archive

Archives often put a limit to the number of loose pages you take into reading rooms where documents are stored, so a spiral bound notebook is very valuable. Number and index the pages for quick reference later. It is better to carry a number of pencils rather than pens. too. Ink can be spilt, even from biros, and archives are keen to preserve their materials. Don't get caught without a writing instrument. An eraser and sharpener are also useful. A few coins should be carried for lockers to store other materials. Some archives permit the use of lap top computers and some now have ports which can be used.

The retrieval of documents will depend very much on the system in operation at each archive, but usually there are catalogues, ledgers, and filing systems to consult. Make a note of the most promising-looking items first. Then list the other items so that you have a systematic coverage of what's on offer. Make your first item request sooner rather than later, as documents can take some time to be brought up from vaults below. Don't forget that the archivists themselves are often knowledgeable on many of the topics you will be studying, and they are always delighted to help people.

Handle materials with care

Documents do not last forever. Even some paper, manufactured a hundred years ago, has begun to deteriorate. Britain has a rich seam of documents, some dating back to the medieval period and it is the historians' responsibility to preserve as much as we can for the future. Archives occasionally restore some items. Frequently-consulted works often appear as microfilm, on tape, or as facsimiles.

If you are lucky enough to see the real thing, you may be presented with a bundle secured with ribbon. Untie and unpack the material carefully. Handle documents slowly. Support book spines and delicate materials with sponge supports. Some archives insist that you wear gloves. Never lean on a document to make notes. Make notes as you read, and don't forget to make a complete record of the code number of each item. Tick off the items as you work through. Be systematic. When you return materials, pack them carefully. Always report damage so that archivists can repair the materials. Enjoy the experience; few can forget the smell of old parchment, the evocative sight of dusty manuscripts, and the excitement of discovering something new, or something old.

Tutorial: helping you learn

Progress questions
1. What functions do AND and OR perform in a Boolean search?

2. What is meant by a gateway site?

3. In what ways can web searches be refined?

Discussion points
Why are electronic sources something that the historian can no longer avoid?

Practical assignment
Compile a bibliography on any historical topic of your choice (perhaps something that you are working on). Add a one-side preface to that bibliography entitled 'Using electronic sources' explaining how you used electronic sources to acquire the bibliography, and the strengths and weaknesses of each method.

Study tips
1. Keep a disk with useful web sites on it. Arrange them into folders by subject.

2. Initiate a disk library of notes and materials. Create subdirectories and folders to keep track of your work.

9

Presentations, Conferences, Workshops and Seminars

One-minute summary – As a historian you must be able to impart your ideas clearly and effectively – not just on paper, but verbally too. Presentations and seminars alike require good preparation, and careful delivery. Rehearsal is essential, to calm nerves and to sound convincing. There is much to be gained from attending seminars and conferences, even ones which are on topics quite unrelated to your own. Keep an open mind and examine the style of delivery and questioning used by others. In this chapter you will learn about:

▶ preparing for and giving seminars

▶ giving effective presentations

▶ making the most of conferences and workshops.

Preparing for and giving seminars

Seminar groups vary in size. Characteristically, they are small groups which give the opportunity to share ideas, and to make sense of the more complex theories and events of history picked up through reading and attending lectures.

The emphasis is on participation. It would be a mistake to believe that a seminar is just another opportunity to listen to a tutor. Try to say something early on, and if neccssary pose a question. Make sure you prepare yourself by doing the 'set reading' before the seminar takes place, and by trying to understand the purpose of the seminar. During the discussion, concentrate on the arguments put forward. Don't worry too much about making notes on factual material. Jot down only the outline of the arguments. Be prepared to justify your own views with solid evidence, too! Seminars are a good opportunity to clarify any difficult sections you are likely to encounter when writing an essay. Make sure you air your doubts about any terms and concepts. Ask questions.

Giving effective presentations

Preparation is the key to success

The secret to a good presentation is preparation. First of all make sure you know exactly what the aim and objectives are of your presentation. What are the terms given? For example:

1. Are you giving a short, ten-minute introduction to a seminar group which wants to know the main themes of a topic and where the contentions lie?

2. Is it a more formal presentation to a group that you do not know, and which does not know much about the topic?

Throughout the preparation, check that you are fulfilling the group's aim and objectives.

Organising your material

A plan, as with an essay, is essential. Once you have decided on your main argument, and supporting arguments, assemble the relevant examples and evidence. Organise your material into a coherent, stage-by-stage argument. Make sure you have smooth linking points. The plan will make a useful introduction so that your listeners will know where you are going.

Be concise. You need to convey your ideas with an economy of effort; both yours and your listeners! Underline or highlight the important points that you want to emphasise. The conclusion should show your understanding, and give points or questions for discussion. Don't pad out your presentation with information the group already knows. Equip yourself with a clear introduction, a main argument supported by evidence, and a convincing conclusion.

Delivery will 'make' your talk

Plan to vary your delivery. The voice can be a wonderful tool; you can speed it up and slow it down for dramatic effect. You can pause prior to an important point to draw attention to it. Think about varying the volume, the rhythm, or the pitch of your voice. You can use arm gestures to reinforce the importance of a point, too. Don't overdo it, but uplifting ideas can be combined with a gracefully raised arm. Thoughtful ideas can be accompanied by placing a hand on your chin. Study how experienced public speakers use gestures, and how comedians use timing. Don't use anecdotes about yourself (too much personality can be as bad as none at all).

Never underestimate the time you will need to prepare and to rehearse. Rehearse thoroughly. Some speakers like to virtually memorise what they will say, others prefer to have a collection of key words on small, unobtrusive cards to jog their memories. Notes are important; never read close-typed material out loud – it will sound flat. The sheets of paper tend to flap around and can be distracting, too.

Practise in front of someone else and ask for some constructive criticism. Any mannerisms (repetitive or distracting habits, like tapping a foot or hanging on to a table like grim death) should be identified. Write reminders on the top of your prompt cards not to do them.

Rehearsal three weeks before a major presentation would not be unreasonable. The more rehearsed, the better prepared you will feel, and the less nervous you will be on the day. Think positively; keep telling yourself that you will be really good and you will!

Making the most of conferences and workshops

Conferences are great places to find out about the latest research, and to hear leading historians discuss their specialisms. It is a great chance to get your questions answered. Conferences often involve a 'chair' speaker who introduces one or more delegates. Each delegate presents a 'paper' which has usually been distributed to the rest of the conference beforehand. If possible, read the paper before the speaker is due to speak. Note briefly anything which appears contentious, and jot down any questions. If the speaker does not address them, you can raise them at the end. Once again, as with the lecture, it is a good idea to focus on the arguments while the speaker gives the paper. If questions are invited, take the opportunity to note the kind of questions that were asked, as well as the answers. Remember these for when you write your own work.

If you are a speaker, consider your audience. You will have to pitch the level and volume of material to suit your listeners. If you receive a challenging question, don't be afraid to acknowledge it as a difficult one. Don't rush into the answer. If you are really stuck you could pass it back to the audience for consideration, as none of us have all the answers. Above all, enjoy the experience; conferences and workshops are a stimulating aspect of the profession.

Tutorial: helping you learn

Progress questions

1. How should you limit the amount of material for a speech?

2. In delivering of your speech, how do you avoid mannerisms?

3. How should you react to difficult questions in a seminar?

Discussion points

'The web will soon make traditional means of delivery for history redundant.' Do you agree?

Practical assignment

Prepare a two-minute talk on yourself. Try not to have too many notes. Use two or three headings which will prompt you to talk about some aspect of your life or beliefs. Two minutes will be up very quickly. Once you have done this, get someone to criticise your performance. Now prepare a five-minute talk on the aspect of history which interests you. Get a debrief on this, too. Finally, attempt to give a ten-minute talk on a more difficult aspect of history – preferably something very contentious.

Study and revision tips

1. Always prepare for conferences, speeches and seminars in advance: you will get more from them.

2. Ask questions, and get assistance from others.

3. Don't be nervous about public speaking, think positively and get as much practical experience as possible.

10

Conclusions

One-minute summary – History is a subject into which we all grow. Ideas are developed through our experience, our reading, and our participation in discussions. By guiding you through the writing of history, you will see the value of the history skills used today. The approach suggested in this Studymate would need to be adapted to the various demands of specialist branches of history, however. Use it as a starting point, a point of departure. This conclusion summarises the key points associated with the business of 'doing history'. In this chapter you will learn about:

▶ the value of studying historiography
▶ the best techniques to improve your performance

The value of studying historiography

A useful vehicle for understanding history

Throughout this Studymate we have suggested that discussion and the sharing of ideas is a valuable means of achieving a better understanding of the past. This is the value of studying historiography, too. History is a subject into which we grow through training and experience. We develop our ideas through reading and taking part in debates. This book has offered a guide to that journey of the writing of history, and ended with the practical business of 'doing history'.

The value of historiography

History is no longer about just politics and the elites who govern and rule. It now embraces the whole range of past human activity. Nor is it a subject concerned with the minutiae of artefacts; that is the province of antiquarians. History is a broader canvas than that. It is a subject that remains sceptical of 'laws of human nature', since so few models of development stand up to historical scrutiny, though it does accept a theoretical framework in some circumstances.

Historical study makes use of all kinds of sources as evidence, but ac-
knowledges the shortcomings both of its evidence and of the historians
themsleves. This is not a disadvantage; in fact, it enriches the subject.
Look again at the Fischer debate and the Gentry debate in chapter
one. These controversies led us to a better understanding of the subject
matter, hard fought as the positions were. Contrast this honest search
for understanding with the blatant dishonesty of some film-makers, or
the propaganda of political extremists.

History was used to convey a message to the present
The classical writers of Greece and Rome reported on near contemporary events in order to draw political lessons, or to present a new account
of some military episode. Herodotus, for example, searched for the
causes of war. Polybius saw history as a tool to improve diplomacy and
politics. Livy developed rhetorical techniques to persuade his audience
of his historical views.

In the so-called Dark Ages, history served a new 'world view' of
Christianity, and of the political authorities in western Europe. The
annals of the medieval period were superseded by the work of Renaissance scholars who used history as the Romans had done – to convey a
message from the past into the present. In doing so, they lost no opportunity to promote the prestige of their own city states and homelands.
History used in this way fostered national and regional identities.

In seventeenth-century England, history was used not simply to
teach school lessons, but to legitimise political power and the rights of
king or parliament. In time, the political settlement was reinforced by
Whig history. There was also a historical idea of progress that demanded to know where the economic success of Britain in the early
nineteenth century originated. The eighteenth-century enlightenment
sought scientific explanations for the universe, including human
nature.'Civilisation' was the ultimate prize if Europe could be successfully re-educated on the basis of 'reason'. Ranke rejected this reliance on
reason and progress. He called for a return to original sources that
would reveal the decision-making of individuals, and offer a glimpse
of what he saw as the real motor of history: the hand of God.

History now broader but specialised
Ranke's contribution to history was both his method and a way of thinking. He called for rigorous training, for detailed and sceptical
documentary analysis, for an understanding that epochs were marked

by different ways of thinking. In fact, he offered an approach that was broader in scope than he has often been credited for. History was thus widened from just politics, and political documents, but it also became more specialised.

Marx contributed a socio-economic analysis of the world. In certain quarters this was found so convincing as to virtually exclude all other factors in historical study. The Annales took a different approach; they aimed to avoid limiting the type and scope of evidence gathered, in order to give an honest picture of a region. The scale was ambitious. The changes they detected, in the 'real' history of the landscape and the masses, were almost imperceptible. Marx's world changed rapidly with violent and bloody revolution, Bloch's changed as slowly as the ox-cart trundling across the vast rolling countryside of rural France. However, in the face of these great, impersonal forces which shaped the world, there seemed little place for individual human intervention. Great events like world wars and an industrial revolution seemed to re-inforce this notion. Inevitably there was a reaction. Historians sought the humanity of history, and began to view the individual as a motor of history.

The most recent challenges have concerned truth

Since the Carr-Elton debate on objectivity, the 'truthfulness' of histor-ians has been debated. While Popper called for history to be used as a defence against totalitarian ideas, literary critics challenged the very basis of how and why historians wrote history at all. History seemed to them little more than a literary flight of fancy, because it was all fiction. But the past *did* happen. The events of the past, their ideas, their lives, *were* real. Historians had never claimed to bring the past back; but they had always maintained they could pass comment on it. Ranke had been misquoted. It had always been 'History as it, essentially, hap-pened'.

The conspiracy theory claimed that historians wanted power, or at least perpetuated the power of a western academic elite through a para-digm of texts and institutions. This theory was soon exposed. It was the post-modernists themselves who wanted power, or to vent their dissatis-faction with the modernist world they inhabited. All too often, though, the post-modernists were forced to acknowledge that the weapons they used were the same as those they attacked. Were it not for the western, liberal, rational tradition, their ideas could not have been expressed that way in the first place. Their insistence that they now owned truth negated their own theory that there was no reality in texts at all.

Nevertheless, it was a valid reminder that historians have to be cautious about texts, and should not place undue emphasis on certain types of history. A string of new histories developed to the great benefit of the subject as a whole. The cross-fertilisation of the disciplines has transformed and widened the range of history to explore all forms of human activity.

History consists of high standards of work and reasoned comment

Historians are no longer simply concerned with events, or with individuals, and the narration of what happened. They are expected to comment upon the past. This commentary must be as objective as possible. Nor should it be so one-sided as to exclude the views of others. Historians must have a good command of their language and of presentation techniques in order to convey their ideas with clarity and efficency. Historians are expected to be aware of other disciplines, and of developments in their own subject through the wide reading of books and journals.

The best techniques to improve your performance

Historical skills

Here is a summary of key skills for historians:

1. Evidence must be presented to authenticate each idea.
2. It is helpful to ask questions at the beginning of the study of a topic, even to form a hypothesis, but the hypothesis must be rigorously tested against the evidence.
3. Be analytical by asking questions, and by adopting an analytical writing style.
4. Remain open to new thoughts. Take part in discussions to exchange ideas.
5. Give yourself thinking time.
6. Read both widely and critically.
7. Be cautious when interrogating all sources.
8. Understand the rules of punctuation, spelling and grammar.
9. Understand the great variety of factors and their relative importance in causation, and in consequences.
10. Be aware of the value of comparative history.

11. Appreciate the different approaches and wide historiography in each topic that you study.

12. Stay current. Be aware of new developments in topics you are studying.

Study skills

Becoming a successful scholar and historian takes effort, but many have achieved a great deal with these fundamental study skills:

1. Get organised with a year planner. Tackle work when it is set; don't let it pile up.

2. Prepare thoroughly for all seminars, lectures and essays.

3. Practise essay-writing, including doing it under timed conditions.

4. Get help if you don't understand something. Don't sit on problems.

5. Learn historical concepts and terms (e.g. socialism, oligarchy, aristocracy, imperialism, relativism, positivism, empiricism, historicism).

6. Rehearse properly before delivering papers, or taking part in seminars.

7. Use electronic sources to acquire information efficiently.

8. Learn how to interrogate documents.

9. Develop an analytical style in the way you read and write history.

10. Stay flexible when preparing for examinations. Exams are designed to test your understanding more than your knowledge.

11. Write at the same time as you read; the act of writing crystallises your thoughts.

12. Enjoy it! History is endlessly interesting, challenging, and relevant to how we live.

Tutorial: helping you learn

Progress questions

1. What was Ranke's contribution to the study of history?

2. What are the drawbacks of a determinist approach to history?

3. What are the strengths and weaknesses of post-modernist criticisms of history?

Discussion questions

1. How modern is our history today?

2. 'It is all very well to talk about cultural history, gender history and social history, but, at the end of the day, the world's events are still driven by the world's leaders and elites.' Is this a valid judgement?

Practical assignment

1. Make a summary list of the main modern historiographical writers and their views. Using two columns, assess their strengths and weaknesses. These notes will not only help you tackle essay questions on the study of history, they will also provide you with interesting comments to make in introductions and conclusions of your work.

2. Read and assess the suggested answers to the sample essay topics in this book.

Study and revision tips

1. Review your notes on the main stages of historiography periodically.

2. Apply the techniques listed in this chapter. For example, be organised and don't sit on problems.

3. Learn the conceptual terms that appear in history and use them in your work.

Sample Essays

Essay 1

Is biography a legitimate form of history?

It is tempting to relegate biography as a lesser form of history because it deals with individuals often as shapers of historical events, and is so focused on one person as to present a partiality which is unrepresentative of the period in which they lived. On the other hand, it cannot be right to claim that individuals are simple factors in other, relentless forces of history. The actions of every individual are not simply the outcome of forces over which they have no control, individuals often reason, calculate, plan and shape their futures. Biography ought to be used as a tool in the process of constructing a wider understanding of a period or historical problem, but like all sources, it should be used with caution.

Genealogists take great pleasure in pursuing their ancestors and their family connections, and extensive use is made of archival material. It is curious that few attempt to place their ancestors in their historical context beyond their immediate locality or family. The biographer may be accused of a similar error. First, they attempt to present a narrow interest, perhaps for a market or audience, in which features of interest are played up, and the 'normal' events are given less emphasis. Second, they are themselves victim to a special interest in their subject, often from a position of some reverence. A notable example here might be the work of C. Headlam on Lord Milner, where the biographer selected documents on Milner which missed out on the more incriminating aspects of Milner's part in engineering the South African War of 1899-1902. D. James wrote a flattering account of Lord Roberts, the commander-in-chief in India (1885-1893) and victor of the same Boer War, and George Seaver, with special access granted by a daughter, wrote a selected biography of the explorer and secret agent, Sir Francis Younghusband.

However, it could be said that all historians are open to the charge of 'special interest' which is, after all, usually why they take up a particular person or period for study. It is this interest and enthusiasm which becomes evident in their work, and sustains them in the rigour of advancing through large numbers of records. Biographers, like historians, perform a valuable service in raising awareness about the life, or lives, of particular individuals. It is for the reader to finally decide on the significance or typicality of the individual, or the part they played in the drama of history. Few would deny the need for biography in the case of those persons who have carried a special responsibility in their lifetime. A history of the mid-seventeenth century would be poorer without the biography of Cromwell: Our Chief of Men (Antonia Fraser), or God's Englishman (Christopher Hill, 1970), or R.S. Paul's Our Lord Protector (1955). The same idea came be applied to other eras. Tudor History without John Guy's Henry VIII, or Nazi Germany without Ian Kershaw's recent Huberis, would be unthinkable.

Taking this final example a stage further, biography serves a vital purpose as long as it is placed in context. Recent studies of Adolf Hitler have placed sensationalist interest on his physical deformities, or on his tortured mind during recuperation in hospital after a British gas attack. Some psychologists have even suggested that his experiences at Passewalk in 1918 actually determined his pathological hatred of the Jews and the Holocaust. A range of historians are regarded as Intentionalist in the historiography of Nazi Germany, but what separates them from the macabre obsessions of the 'sensationalists', is the fact that they place Hitler in the context of his time and place. Hitler was not propelled into power until 1933, but his pathological hatred was not so irrational that he became a criminal responsible for killing Jews himself. He was a politician who exploited opportunities that arose in the special, even unique, circumstances of the Depression in the 1930's. There was nothing inevitable about his selection as Chancellor. Historians therefore place Hitler back in the environment of Germany in the 1920's, which helps to explain his particular ideas and why he enjoyed the sympathy of a growing number of Germans from a remarkable cross-section of society. Whilst Lucy Dawidowicz would argue that Hitler intended there to be various outcomes to his regime, not least the destruction of Jewish-Bolshevism, another school of historians argue that there were no planned outcomes. Indeed, these 'functionalists' stress that the chaotic, polycratic division of power in Nazi Germany produced the destruction of Jews as a result of competing groups trying to work to the perceptions of what the Fuhrer's agenda might be. It was the lack of strong leadership that allowed the regime to lurch into the extreme policies of the Holocaust. It is precisely this debate which would not occur in a pure biography. Consequently it is the need for a context which makes a wider history a more suitable vehicle for understanding the past.

After the death of Charles I in 1649, his last words and the dignity of his passing inspired a cult of his martyrdom at the hands of the radicals in London. The passages he is alleged to have written, entitled Eikon Basillica, were popular, and at least went some way to paving the way for a popular restoration despite the power of the army and Cromwell's agents to prevent the passage of pro-Royalist propaganda. Biography is a popular part of the sale of monographs, and the popularity of certain historical figures can be used as a political tool. David Cannadine has recently written a series of essays on Britain and its monarchy, and perhaps the strength of his work for posterity, over Andrew Morton's work on the late Princess of Wales, it is that it will serve to pass a commentary on the context of Diana. In isolation, Morton's work will be viewed as an observation of a sad member of the royal family, but Cannadine can explain the significance of the huge outpourings of national grief at her funeral and the varied expressions of public feeling during her life and death. Ironically, because of the strength of biography as a medium, it is undoubtedly Morton's book that will outsell the 'history'. Biography is thus a legitimate, if dangerous and potential misleading, form of history that, whilst popular, often lacks the setting in which the character lived.

Essay 2

'War is the locomotive of history'. Do you agree?
Despite Lenin's confident statement, such an extreme interpretation of the mechanism of history is misleading, although it makes a refreshing change to the usual Marxist doctrine of historical materialism. More recently, Professor Jeremy Black (Why Wars Happen, 1998) had asserted that war is a product of man's bellicosity, or a propensity to violence, based on rational, and irrational, calculation. In this sense, we might suggest that the driving force of history is little more than an urge to violence, and an inevitable outcome of human existence. On the other hand, we would be wielding a pretty blunt axe in this respect, and we would be open to the charge of making anthropological generalisations and applying them to history. Instead, we could suggest that von Clausewitz was more accurate when he stated that war was 'the extension of politics by other means'. In this definition, we might argue that

war and politics were mechanisms of history since they are concerned with decision-making, and this, rather than just warfare, is a convincing explanation of how 'history happens'.

Since the 1960s political and constitutional history has been less predominant. It is has given way to new studies in social history, economic history, and more recently, the development of local, cultural and gender history. These new histories have opened fresh perspectives on the 'mechanisms' of history. For example, demographic pressures and the shift to greater urbanisation in early nineteenth century Britain, had huge consequences for an economic take-off in the industrial revolution. Similarly, the preceding agricultural revolution made the industrial revolution possible. In economic history, historians will draw attention to the development of a mercantilist system into a capitalist one at the end of the fifteenth century in western Europe, as a the mechanism of change in history generally. They might also highlight the causes of European colonial expansion in the nineteenth century as the product of capitalist entrepreneurs who sought to acquire cheap raw materials and wider markets for their goods, an idea which has been around since the publication of Hobson (1902) and Schumpeter (1919). Spiralling labour costs, and the staking out of territories and consumers for future development by other Europeans, fostered a spirit of competition and insecurity at the end of the 1800s. Few would deny the dynamism of such a period, yet its wars were small and merely the outcomes of other factors, mainly the driving force of economics. If the development of technology was used as a index of economic change then, in Europe, this was indeed a rapid and far-reaching shift.

In cultural history, emphasis is often placed on literature and ideas as motivating factors for change. In one recent example, Edward Said (Orientalism, 1978) maintained that Europeans constructed a web of discourse that subordinated the Egyptians so persuasively, that the indigenous peoples own culture was deeply affected by it. The Europeans sought to acquire knowledge of a culture, but also to perpetuate their own interpretation of it, in order to render it subordinate. The battle to cast off European culture in the Middle East sometimes appears to have encouraged a militant form of Islamic Fundamentalism, and the cultural history of the region cannot ignore a struggle of ideology as readily as other realms of history.

However, it could be argued that one of the factors which accelerates all other processes of history is warfare. Any struggle between organised groups represents an extreme form of competition, and since survival is often involved, the keenest competitiveness is found. For example, huge leaps forward in relatively short periods of time are made in weapons technology. This has a corresponding spin-off in other areas. In the Second World War, the development of faster aircraft led to the introduction of jet aircraft in the RAF, when only 4 years before, its naval aviation, the Fleet Air Arm, had gone to war flying bi-planes that were little more than versions of the aircraft used in the First World War. The tank also enjoyed significant development in the few years of the Second World War, after little progress in the peacetime of the 1920's and 1930's. Arguably, Germany was the only exception here, but it could be posited that the Nazi regime was ahead precisely because it was gearing up for war from 1933.

However, the rapidity of development in wartime does not simply concern technology. It could be argued that during the early seventeenth century there was little change in the actual weaponry the soldiers used, but tactics evolved significantly. The Spanish Tercio has traditionally been regarded as an obsolete formation compared with the linear tactics used by the Swedish and the Dutch at battles such as Lutzen. The 'Military Revolution' debate made much of the introduction of more mobile artillery, and the greater use of musketeers at the expense of pikemen, and attributed these innovations to the more enlightened 'reformer' states of northern Europe. This view, proposed by Parker, has since been revised by Parrott and Black. Historians now recognise that ideas developed on both sides with equal rapidity in response to each new campaign.

The French revolution was regarded by the intellectuals of the nineteenth century as one of the most important events of the modern age. It introduced new ideas, it was thought, and carried them across the face of Europe, and its effects were still being felt in the Bolshevik revolution in 1917. Yet the revolution in France did not invent the ideas with which it has been so long associated. The libertarian notions expressed as the slogans fraternité, egalité, and liberté had already featured in the American War of Independence, and Tom Paine and Samuel Adams had uttered them long before Lafayette, Robespierre or Danton. The new legal codes and systems of government were experiments which were carried to other states by conquest. The French Revolutionary wars, and subsequently the campaigns of Napoleon, were the vehicles by which the ideas were transferred to the rest of the continent. The survival of the ideas, and their spread during the nineteenth century is not denied, but there still had to be the defining moment of conflict when groups or social classes who espoused these new liberal ideas had to confront the Ancien Regime in battle. The revolutions of 1848, and the counter-attacks that followed were still the 'locomotives of history'.

The assertion then, that war is the locomotive of history is too deterministic and mechanistic to apply to every aspect of the past. But it is not a statement without some considerable validity. Episodes of warfare had thrust forward new ideas, stimulated technological development, focused the decision-making of polities, and even enabled the European commercial entrepreneurs to establish their colonies successfully in the nineteenth century, and therefore, we must acknowledge war as one of the most dynamic and catalysing factors of our heritage. War does not do this solely, but any history that ignores its effects neglects to acknowledge this fundamental truth of the past.

Checklist: Framing a historical enquiry

General questions to ask

1. What problem needs to be solved? (Define the historical problem as a question.)

2. What is the existing scholarship? (What work has already been carried out in this field? Are there works which must be consulted? What are the existing controversies? What omissions are there in this field? What can other disciplines offer in the investigation of this problem?)

3. What sources are required/available? What are the gaps? (Where are the sources, and is there access to them? Are there sources which are unavailable?)

4. What depth of enquiry is required? (What timescale is required? What will be the starting point and end point? What level of detail will be needed?)

5. How is the information to be presented? (Is this to be a seminar paper, a book, a journal article, an essay?)

Questions to ask of documents

1. Who wrote it? (What do we know of the background of the author?)

2. When was it written? (What else was happening then?)

3. Why was it written? (Were there any special circumstances surrounding it?)

4. Who was it written for? (For whom was it intended?)

5. What does it say? (Describe its contents, message and hidden meanings.)

6. What doesn't it say? (What does it leave unsaid? Was this omission deliberate?)

7. What other sources do we have to compare it with? (Can we corroborate its themes?)

8. Is it typical? (If it is exceptional, does it have validity?)

9. Is it reliable? (If unreliable, does it still tell us something about the past?)

10. What use is it to the historian? (Is it significant? Does it tell us something which is important?)

Web Sites for History Students

The internet, or world wide web, is a wonderful resource, giving the student nearly free and almost immediate information on almost any topic. Historiography is not, as yet, a subject with a vast amount of coverage on the world wide web. However, there are a number of sites which do assist with the study of history. Below is a selection of the most useful. Please note that neither the author nor the publisher is responsible for content or opinions expressed on the sites listed, which are simply intended to offer starting points for students. Also, please remember that the internet is a fast-changing environment, and links may come and go. If you have some favourite sites you would like to see in future editions of this book, please write to Dr Robert Johnson, c/o Studymates (address on back cover), or email him at the address below. You will find a free selection of useful and readymade student links at the Studymates web site. Happy surfing!

http://www.studymates.co.uk
robertjohnson@studymates.co.uk

Historiography

Historiography
http://english-server.hss.cmu.edu/history/
This is a really good site, with a list of useful historiographical topics.

History and Theory
http://www.wesleyan.edu/histjrnl/hthome.htm
This site covers history and theory, with information on current debates.

World History Archives
http://www.hartford-hwp.com/archives/10/index.html
This is a world history archives site, which covers historiography.

History of history writing
http://www.unifi.it/riviste/cromohs/
Here is another site covering the history of the writing of history. There are links to other sites of interest for historians at /sites.html.

Ranke

Ranke
http://www.lib.byu.edu/-rah/prmss/n-r/ranke.html
This site is dedicated to Leopold von Ranke. Some of the material is in
German.

Ricci on Ranke
http://www.nhumanities.org/ricci.htm
The content of this web site is related to the issues that Ranke raised on
God's role in history. Gabriel Ricci examines the part played by metaphysics and history in an essay.

Annales
http://info.lib.uh.edu/wj/webjour.htm
The site presents a list of scholarly journals distributed via the web, with
links to the Annales.

Marxist history

The Institute of Historical Research
http://ihr.sas.ac.uk/ihr/bbs.ihr.html
This is site of the Institute of Historical Research with links to the
various strands of the discipline, from world history to local history.
You will find information on educational sites, recent publications,
PhDs in history, and very much more. Excellent.

History Online
http://www.historyonline.ac.uk
This is a subscription site organised by the Historical Association.

Further Reading

Studying history

J. Black and Donald McCraild, *Studying History* (Macmillan, 1997 2nd edition, 2000). This guide is perhaps the most similar to this one in the sense that it sets out the history of history, before tackling 'how to do history' in the second half. However, it has no self-test questions, sample answers or essay guidance notes. It has not been too popular with students, mainly due to an unattractive layout (dense, long chapters), even though the content is comprehensive.

John Warren, *History and the Historians* (Hodder & Stoughton, 1998). The access to history series was much heralded by A-level history teachers as ideal for A-level students, and this book would, no doubt, appeal to the same readers. It deals solely with historiography and covers all the major debates in a clear format. It is not really a study guide, and comes across as Warren's own view. There is a brief coverage of a solution to the historiographical maze that is thrown up, but it is difficult to follow, and buried in a colloquial, conversational style. An original attempt at opening the minds of today's historians by means of interview transcripts appeared in an edition of the book called *The Past and its Presenters*. However, this didn't really work: their ideas are too difficult to access quickly; you have to wade through the whole book to make it work. There are also gaps (there is nothing on the seventeenth century or anything outside of Europe and the United States – as if they didn't exist). However, the coverage of the Marxist interpretation of history is clear and easy to understand.

Gilbert Pleuger, ed., *The Good History Student's Handbook* (Sempringham Studies, 1997). Following the launch of Sempringham's *New Perspective Magazine*, the collected articles of advice on studying history formed this book. It was aimed solely at the A-level market but was not generally purchased by students. The chapters were fine as journal articles but perhaps suffered by being squeezed into one volume. However, the chapter headings are clear and deal with the difficult skills. No historiography was included at all.

Gordon Taylor, *The Student's Writing Guide* (Arts and Social Sciences). (Cambridge, 1989). Strictly speaking, this is a style manual, but the opening chapters cover writing essays, and there is a useful, plain English, explanation on how to write, read, take notes, be analytical and even how to write a book review. The size, bold title, and price make this book useful, and it can be used instead of the 'official' post-graduate style manuals (known as MHRA and MRA).

Historiography
Richard Evans, *In Defence of History* (1998). This is by far the best account of the recent crisis in history and a practical, positive approach to its resolution.

Keith Jenkins, *Re-Thinking History* (1991). Jenkins called for a new ap-proach to history which encompasses all aspects of the discipline and which was more honest. Thought-provoking at the time of its publica-tion.

Arthur Marwick, *The Nature of History* (reprinted, 1989). This is still one of the most articulate works of defence for the traditional historical method. Marwick gives an overview of historiography and a common-sense practical guide to the historian's craft.

Marxism
David McLellen, *Karl Marx* (1976). This is still one of the best accounts of Marx's life and works. It includes extracts of Marx's thoughts on history. H.J Kaye, *British Marxist Historians* (1984) is the definitive study of this group.

Annales
Peter Burke, *The French Historical Tradition: the Annales School, 1929-1989* (1990). This is the best explanation of the thinking behind the Annales approach.

New histories
One of the best overviews of the emergence of new history is Peter Burke, *New Perspectives on Historical Writing* (1991), but such a diverse field requires further research.

Local history

A useful starting point for local history would be Robert Dunning, *Local History for Beginners* (1973) and W. G. Hoskins, *Fieldwork in Local History* (1967).

Women's history

The best introduction to this subject is J. W. Scott, *Gender and the Politics of History* (1988).

Glossary

Aufklärer Philosophers of the Enlightenment (German)

deconstruction The process of explaining the implied meaning of a text; a way of revealing the author's true intentions.

determinism The dogmatic notion that events or processess always follow a pattern.

discourses An accumulation of writing

document question Here, one or more extracts from original sources are presented along with a series of questions for the student to answer.

economic determinism The idea that all human activity is dictated by economics.

empiricism The process of producing an analysis based on evidence.

ethnocentrism Centring on, or defined, by ethnicity or race.

historical materialism A Marxist belief that history is driven by the materialistic concerns of economics; such as property, profit and competition.

historicism Either (1) the idea that the past cannot be understood without reference to present day ideas and values, or (2) that there are laws of history which undermine the role of human free will, or (3) nostalgia for the past.

historiography Either (1) the way that history has been written, or (2) the philosophy of history.

inter-textuality The idea that historical texts were simply the results of other texts

meta-narrative A form of history which is governed by laws of development; for example, Marxist history.

metaphysics Ideas that apparently cannot be proved or disproved, such as the existence of God.

methodological individualism The name given to Karl Popper's rejection of determinism in history.

mnemonics an ancient system of remembering lists of information using the first letter of each item in the list and assembling a new word from them.

Namierisation The process of meticulous historical research associated with Lewis Namier.

objectivity The idea that historians can be impartial in assessing the past.

paradigm a well-known example

philosophes Philosophers of the Enlightenment (French).

plagiarism The academic fraud of lifting of whole lines, passages, or even ideas of another writer, without acknowledging the source. The theft of intellectual property.

positivism The idea that an understanding of the past offers a chance to know the future, or the idea that every aspect of the human condition can be scientifically tested or understood.

post-modernism A philosophical idea that rejected science, rationality and progress as misleading propaganda.

post-structuralism A rejection of the idea that text has objective meaning.

prospography A collection of biographies.

relativism An inappropriate comparison, usually determining that one example is better than another.

search string A term in electronic information retrieval. It means the key words you choose, when searching for information, which most approximate to your topic of interest.

structural analysis An absolute reliance on archival research and painstaking care in documentary analysis, a technique developed by Lewis Namier.

taxonomy Classification, stereotyping.

total history An attempt to include all factors of human activity into a history, rather than limiting it to a study of politics. Associated with the Annales.

Suggested abbreviations for history notes

Latin abbreviations

circa [c.]	about
c.f.	compare
e.g.	for example
c.p.	contrast
q.v.	refer to
viz.	see
ff.	following (pages)

English abbreviations

b.	born
d.	died
m.	married
ed.	edited by
no.	number

Some useful historical abbreviations

C19	nineteenth century
Ind. Rev.	Industrial Revolution
Govt.	government
Parlt.	parliament
Prot./R.C.	Protestant/Roman Catholic
Med.	medieval
Emp.	empire
Soc.	society/social

Index